Secret Stories of Leadership, Growth, and Innovation

Sustainable Transformation for a Safer, New, and Better World

BY DAVID RADLO

Table of Contents

DEDICATION

Growing up right after the Great Depression, part of the "Greatest Generation," my mom, Irene, or "Renie," worked seven jobs to put herself through UMass. One of those positions was teaching high school history. For graduate school, she commuted to the Harvard-affiliated Radcliffe Management Training Program in Cambridge, MA. She was a strong advocate for gender integration into Harvard Business School, which admitted women within a decade or so after her graduation. Later, she received bank credit training and joined my father as a full partner in their business.

My mom was undoubtedly the most intelligent and respectful finance professional I have ever met. She was a fabulous teaching mother and grandmother. Although you will find some of the accomplishments of my father, Jason, or "Jack," from WWII and beyond in this book, Jack also found time to go to every sports game and activity for both me and my children, Ben and Jessica, as they grew up. Dad was a wonderful father and grandfather. Here's to your living memory, Mom and Dad, with sincere appreciation for your sacrifices.

FOREWORD

Organizational excellence occurs when a growth mindset is applied to proven internal and external practices to operate efficiently while meeting or exceeding delivery standards. David Radlo and I share a passion for organizational excellence and feel strongly about giving back locally and nationally to sustainably encourage a safer, more equitable, and better world. I have known Dave Radlo for several years through our mutual support of our alma mater, Tufts University, and the Carson Scholars Fund. Our common interests of entrepreneurship, education, and social innovation have culminated in mutual respect and friendship. I was honored and humbled when David asked me to be a part of his latest journey, *Secret Stories of Leadership, Growth, and Innovation*.

As a cofounder and partner at FVLCRUM Funds, a community development and public welfare equity investment firm based in Washington, DC, I have been engaged in social entrepreneurship for nearly a decade. Focusing on creating both impact and top quartile market returns, the firm exclusively invests in minority-owned businesses to create generational wealth for the executive teams and substantial economic opportunities for minorities and low–moderate-income communities. FVLCRUM is one of the few minority-owned private investment firms in the country and was established to intentionally address the racial wealth gap, which we believe to be the defining issue of our generation. Over the past eight years, our companies have created several thousand jobs in underserved areas and created substantial wealth for minorities while achieving over 900% return on invested capital. I am convinced that innovative capital structures and dedication to driving top market returns can be combined with commonsense strategies to sustainably solve critical societal issues and become permanent fixtures in the capital markets.

Prior to cofounding FVLCRUM, I served six years at the Warner Companies, where I advised companies on mergers and acquisitions, capital structuring, capital raises, investments, risk management, and strategic planning. Ultimately, I became one of the executive vice presidents of the company, leading the alternative investment division and working directly with the CEO and other division heads. The company had an intense focus on operational excellence and was a tremendous foundation builder early in my career.

Outside of my profession, I remain active in community, political, and meaningful business initiatives. I have been involved in several political efforts, including serving on the board of Carson America, the presidential campaign of Dr. Benjamin Carson. Other board engagements include the President's Council at Tufts University, Young Presidents Organization, Charge Enterprises (stock: CRGE), the Minority Wealth Commission, and the Carson Scholars Fund. I have found that these and other boards allow me to stay focused on supporting my core passions of education, entrepreneurship, workforce development, and minority- and women-owned businesses.

I am honored to have been a 2019 AEI Scholar, as well as a recipient of Baltimore's 35 Under 35 award, the Envest Foundation's 40 Under 40 award, *Franchise Journal's* MBE Titans, Washington Life's 40 Under 40, and DCA Rising Stars of GovCon.

As previously noted, Dave and I share a common purpose of delivering sustainable leadership through commercial endeavors and meaningful civic engagement to create a safer, more equitable, and better world. Leadership in this manner includes working with government agencies, political systems, and industry partners to realize sustainable objectives, including using your time, talents, and money for what matters most, which David has done many times.

David has been exceedingly successful at growing, acquiring, operating, and exiting businesses in consumer product food and beverage, agriculture, franchise, and biotech. He has also been involved in technology and consumer entertainment and media, private equity, and early-stage ventures. At his heart, and as a 3X Entrepreneur himself, David is a passionate expert in leadership, innovation, and expansion who has driven business and market growth by double- and, at times, triple-digit CAGRs (compounded annual growth rate), utilizing both organic and inorganic strategies. Having executed nearly $2.3B in M and A transactions, David shares his experiences as an industry-leading CEO, Trusted Advisor, board member, growth and exit coach, Fortune 500 speaker, best-selling author, and podcaster in pursuit of leaving the world in a better place than where he found it.

David has an uncanny ability to uncover the X factor that leads to organizational excellence, which grew his companies by 3X, 5X, and 30X enterprise value, and he enjoys helping others do the same. He can envision synergistic partnerships, alliances, and strategic investments to maximize value and purpose for people and companies. His ability to communicate through the lens of his own success has allowed him to share his expertise at scale, helping many executives better navigate the challenges of corporate growth, operational improvements, capital markets access, and building toward the successful sale of a business.

In *Secret Stories*, David gives a rare glimpse into commercial negotiations, international relations, and successful back-channel diplomacy with former Cuban dictator Fidel Castro. He details his constructive engagement efforts for economic means with a focus on local and worldwide sustainability, environmental social governance, education, and security. Further, David reflects on the lessons from his first book, *Principles of Cartel Disruption: Accelerate and Maximize Performance*, and his podcast, *Sustainable Leadership and Disruptive Growth*, aligning third-party narratives with his own real-life situations.

He also provides insight from doing business (and battles) with cartels, showcasing how it is essential to understand the difference between a cartel mindset and a disruptive mindset when maximizing growth. *Secret Stories* is a first-hand account of how multibillion-dollar industries are built, the real-life, ongoing wars between organized commerce and special interest groups from the smoke-filled backrooms, and how to deal with discrimination head on in true "cartel-disruptor" style. At the end of the book, David adds a never-before-revealed 12th Principle to chew on: "Understand the Cartel Leadership Rules."

Every chapter is insightful and straightforward, with newly revealed negotiations and assessments of events, secrets, and hidden lessons learned. *Secret Stories of Leadership, Growth, and Innovation—Sustainable Transformation for a Safer, New, and Better World*, is an extraordinarily engaging, exciting, and riveting pragmatic educational ride and quite humorous at times. It's a must-read, and I gladly endorse this fabulous book!

Benjamin S. Carson Jr.

INTRODUCTION

Are you interested in knowing what it's like to deal with Fidel Castro, free dissident prisoners through back-channel diplomacy, or build a billion-dollar specialty egg market of Eggland's Best, Born Free, Free Range, and Organic? How about how we became cage-free and an alternative protein nation? Would you like to learn about the business rationale for local golf club alleged discrimination and how to handle it Cartel Disruptor Style? What about learning the Secret and Hidden Cartel Leadership Rules? How about ways to give back with time, talent, contacts, and finance to sustainably transform for a safer, new, and better world?

Welcome to *Secret Stories of Leadership, Growth, and Innovation-Sustainable Transformation for a Safer, New, and Better World*. It's my first-hand account of how multibillion-dollar categories and industries are built and how organized commerce and special interest groups battle. One of the key themes of this book is showcasing how 'effective' leadership resulted in billions earned and how 'ineffective' leadership resulted in missed opportunities and disaster.

I follow up the 11 Principles of Leadership, Growth, and Innovation found in the first book, *The Principles of Cartel Disruption*, and add a twelfth secret and hidden key principle (See Exhibit I1). I take you behind the curtain and give you a rare glimpse into commercial negotiations and successful back channel diplomacy with former Cuban dictator Fidel Castro and focus on local and worldwide effective sustainability and Environmental Social Governance (ESG).

Focusing on the difference between a disruptive mindset and a cartel and market leader mindsets, I reflect on the lessons from Cartel Disruption and my Forbesbooks radio podcast, *Sustainable Leadership, and Disruptive Growth*, aligning third-party narratives with real-life situations. I detail the greatest strategic planning and execution mistake in food and agricultural consumer product marketing history and give you the details of a roller coaster ride in exiting the business.

Strap on your seatbelt! Enjoy the ride.

Exhibit I1. 12 Principles Found in Principles of Cartel Disruption (+ the New 12th Principle)

SECTION 1 - MARKET RESEARCH AND VALUE PROPOSITION

Principle I: Understand Your Opportunity and Create a Winning Value Proposition.

SECTION 2 - FUNDING

Principle II: Design and Deliver a Pitch that Secures Funding.

Principle III: Understand the Basic Legal Game, Documents for Funding, and Legalities for Intellectual Property Protection.

SECTION 3 - OPERATIONAL EXCELLENCE

Principle IV: Develop a Sound and Thorough Strategic Plan in Order to Succeed.

Principle V: Clearly Understand and Utilize People Resources.

Principle VI: Design and Improve Efficient and Effective Core Processes.

Principle VII: Learn and Implement the Power of Sustainability and Environmental Social Governance.

Principle VIII: Use Operational Metrics to Guide Your Test Marketing and Early-Stage Milestones.

Principle IX: Understand Your Exit Opportunities and Develop a Strategy to Make It Happen.

Principle X: Select a Talented Board of Directors and Advisors to Help Accelerate Growth Based upon the Needs of the Business.

SECTION 4 - GIVING BACK

Principle XI: Understand the Importance of Giving Back with 1) Time and Talents, 2) Sharing Your Network of Contacts and Direct Opportunities, and 3) Financial Resources.

SECTION 5 - NEW SECRET AND HIDDEN PRINCIPLE

Principle XII: Understand the Cartel Leadership Rules (Written and Unwritten Versions)

CHAPTER ONE

Breaking into the Country Cartel: Cuba

"The mob owned Cuba . . . and then lost it to the revolution."
- T. J. English.

In 2002, Fidel Castro laid it on the line to me in a personal discussion that made me reflect on whether Socialism and Marxism were ends in themselves or means for a cartel takeover and control of power. We will explore this further as we go deeper in the book. Castro told me, "Daveed, Harvard did not give me a scholarship, so I went to Columbia. I then left to go to Cuba and took over a country. Daveed, do you think I made the right decision? What do you think of my costs? What do you think of my market share? One hundred percent of everything. No Sherman Act. No Clayton Act. And total control of the army, politics, and business."

For those that may wonder how I was introduced to Fidel Castro, I'll let you in on the introduction and then go into more depth as we dive deeper into the book. I went down to Havana on a trade mission with Jim Sumner, president and CEO of the USA Poultry and Egg Export Council (USAPEEC), and Greg Tyler, the de facto COO of the operation, as well as the chicken boys and girls from Tyson, Perdue, and Pilgrim's Pride, Allied Turkey, which included Don DeLordo of Michigan Turkey, who paved the road for Joel Coleman and Butterball and others. Jim Hoban was a chicken exporter and a great guy to have on these trips. Although the money was usually not as much, export trips were a great time when Jim Sumner was there. John Hampton, a board member, expert at structuring financial deals and friend since NYU Stern Business School, accompanied me on this trip.

Fidel Castro and the Cuba Years

Cuba has arguably been a fertile ground for cartels. The US mob operated under Fulgencio Batista's rule supported by the US government, and now, Cuba is controlled by the Castro family. There's been a lot written about Cuba, the fantastic culture, the Cuban-American relationship, the US trade embargo, and travel restrictions to the country. But, most of all, there has been a focus on Fidel Castro de Ruz, his family and compatriots, the revolution that he pioneered, his personal charisma, and the leadership that he invoked through a combination of nationalism, support for Marxist-Leninist Socialism, and ruthless intolerance for dissent.

I promise you, after getting to know Cuba well over trips spanning more than a decade and a half and about a dozen or so meetings with Castro, I got a first-class glimpse of Cuba. Nothing embodied the revolution more than a speech that was made famous several years ago when Castro was imprisoned by the government of Fulgencio Batista.

During his trial, on September 16, 1953, he gave a speech entitled "History Will Absolve Me," which ended up being the blueprint of the reasons for a revolution. Castro referenced Dante: "Dante divided his hell into nine circles. He put the criminals in the seventh, the thieves in the eighth, and the traitors in the ninth. What a hard dilemma the devil will face when he must choose the circle adequate for the soul of Batista." Later Castro spoke to me about an American president in a fiery hour-long address with his security guards locked and loaded nearby.

T. J. English noted in his book *Havana Nocturne*, "The mob owned Cuba and lost it to the Revolution." Castro quoted from several sources, including St. Thomas Aquinas, Jean-Jacques Rousseau, Honoré de Balzac, Thomas Paine, and José Martí, the benevolent nineteenth-century Cuban leader. Castro put forth evidence for a revolution to the Cuban people. They suffered infinite misfortune as a result of Cuba's failures of land distribution, housing, education, unemployment, civic corruption, political repression, and the economic plundering of the island and redistribution of the loot by outside forces.

Further, Castro addressed his own predicament by stating, "I know I shall be silenced for many years. I know that they will try to conceal the truth by every possible means, but my voice will never be drowned, for it gathers strength within my breast when I feel alone. I know that prison will be harder for me than it has ever been for anyone, filled with threats, vileness, and cowardly cruelty. But I do not fear prison, as I do not fear the fury of the miserable tyrant who snuffed out the lives of seventy of my comrades. Condemn me. It does not matter. History will absolve me." Castro was then sentenced to fifteen years in prison and Batista later made the biggest mistake in his life and let him out so that he could carry out a revolution and take over the Cuban cartel.

Some of the outside forces were the boys in organized crime from the United States that grew the gaming business and nightclubs. Havana was roaring with gambling, shows, hotels, and all things entertainment. At the center of this was the Jewish and Italian mob led in Cuba by Meyer Lansky.

In 1946, at the Hotel Nacional, the famous mob conference was held that set up the seed money and the strategy for organized crime in Cuba. They came from Buffalo, New York City, Chicago, Cleveland, and from the states of New Jersey, Louisiana, and Florida. Vito Genovese, Meyer Lansky, Santo Trafficante, Carlos Marcello, and Frank Costello, who was tied into Lucky

Luciano, who had been sent elsewhere by the authorities. Meyer Lansky was the financier, and he stayed in the background, but he was the man with the plan. The goal was to build a Cuban-based Monte Carlo, and boy, did they ever.

They built quite an empire while building the relationship between the US and Cuba, including a government partnership with dictator Fulgencio Batista. Batista quietly earned kickbacks and was the ultimate partner with the mob and Cuba. He was also backed by the United States government. At the end of the day, Fidel Castro bankrupted Lansky and the mob in Cuba with the takeover of the island and shutting down the gambling casinos in 1959. In *Principles for Cartel Disruption*, the first strategic planning trap was to *"fail to recognize and understand events and changing conditions in the competitive environment."* It was as if they did not see it coming.

In 1955, Castro found it hard to hide his contempt for the Cuban nightlife that was attracting tourists from around the world.

"What does our homeland's pain and people's touring matter to the rich and fatuous who fill the dance halls?" he said. "For them, we are unthinking young people, disturbers of the existing social paradise. There will be no lack of idiots who think we envy them and aspire to the same miserable idle and reptilian existence they enjoy today."[1]

Castro was referring to the sexual degradation of the Cuban citizens for the entertainment of North American and European tourists, which was the dirty little secret of the Havana mob. Notwithstanding, Castro benefited from the hotels and other assets that the mob had built for free with the takeover. Regardless, the sound of Afro-Cuban jazz and traditional sounds that played in the barrios and music halls were an extraordinary draw to all citizens.

However, Fidel did not see that he was in control of everything on the island. I found that quite interesting. When it came to Ernest Hemingway, he considered him to be in literature at the level Fidel was in terms of ownership and politics. "We knew of each other and saw each other at fishing competitions at times, but we generally coexisted," Castro said. He did not have an issue with Hemingway's fame and actually quite appreciated it and never saw Hemingway as a political or economic threat.

In essence, the revolution was an improvised entrepreneurship model. It cracked and disrupted the Batista mob cartel and took it over based upon *socialismo o muerte* (socialism or death). This is in the same vein as in the American Revolution era when Patrick Henry cried, "Give me liberty or give me death!" or Benjamin Franklin said, "We must hang together, or we surely will hang separately."

Some of the movement's biggest events, like the attack of the barracks at Moncada and the landing of the boat *Granma*, which was a failed strike, initially felt like defeats. But the 26th of July Movement had a way of rallying these defeats and cries that led to victory later. The team of the Castros, Guevara, and William Gálvez targeted as the revolution continued not just Batista but also the historical treatment of plundering in Cuba. It was an inevitable process of "*socialismo o muerte.*"[2]

Entrepreneurship Disruption to Cartel Takeover and Challenges to Possible Disruptors

Cuba went through different periods after the takeover. The initial period included the commencement of the embargo by President Kennedy and then the CIA failed attack by Cuban-American forces at the Bay of Pigs. The Cuban Missile Crisis involved high-stakes drama between the US and the Soviets over missiles in Cuba. This was part of the solidification with the Soviet Communist-Leninist partnership that bolstered strong economic ties with its satellite regime. Then, there was the establishment of the US Interests Section at the Swiss Embassy in Havana by President Carter, which was the first step in restoring diplomatic relations between the US and Cuba.

Later, when the Soviet Union crumbled, they couldn't afford to fund Cuba and other satellite nations, so Cuba had to find other ways to fund its nation. Cuba was forced to moderate its hardline Communist-Socialist stance and attract tourism and other revenue to the island as the nation approached the new millennium. They used cartel tactics to maximize cash flow and maintain control through methods like tourist apartheid by a dollar economy. It was utilized with Western hard currency and a peso economy for the locals. There were also restrictions on locals mixing with foreigners, except for the people working to service them.

Marc Frank, in *Cuban Revelations*, characterizes this time, when he returned to Cuba in 1993 after a few years hiatus, as blackout: "Cuba was bankrupt, and I landed in a world that resembled a national disaster or a war. Gross Domestic Product (GDP) was off by 35%, industrial production and agricultural supplies were off by 80%, and foreign trade was off by 75%."

The populace *took it on the chin from a lack of food and medical supplies. During this time, Castro planned for an emerging economy, so he relaxed the opportunity for people to get hard currency from their relatives in the US and started working on tourist development.*[3]

Things got ugly when ferryboats headed to the US were hijacked. Cuban exile groups allegedly machine-gunned hotels and tourists and planted a bomb in the Hotel Capri lobby right near the Hotel Nacional in 1997. People had a hard time making ends meet, and there was a lot of creativity in trying to get through a diet that was diminishing. To bring aid, Castro relaxed the restriction on religion in the country and allowed the active practice of it, according to Frank.

Under President Bill Clinton, the TSRA was put forth, and US agriculture and medicine could once again sell to Cuba. Thank you, President Clinton and the US Congress for allowing us to participate as a supplier to this major cartel nation.

Regardless of what anyone may claim in firebrand speeches from the US or Cuba, I see the situation as being Humpty-Dumpty sitting in the middle of the fence during the longest-running divorce battle between families. The situation pits the Cuban regime against the South Florida and New Jersey Cuban-American interest groups and their political representatives, with some of the leaders having direct family ties. Anyone who says anything to the contrary is not effectively dealing with it. Based upon personal experience, the greatest argument that is espoused by Cuban Americans not to settle this dispute is, "What would my parents or grandparents think?" The younger generations, although more open to changing the situation, still have a deep respect for older hardline policies against liberalization with regard to Cuba and remain in a state of cold war.

The US has failed to foment revolution despite numerous attempts over several decades by presidents based upon the requests of Cuban Americans, including through the use of radio transmissions that have been successful in Eastern Europe. Further, kingdoms and autocracies have fallen in Tunisia, Egypt, Yemen, Syria, Libya, and other Middle Eastern and North African kingdoms and autocracies. Frank addresses the reasons for the failure:[4]

There is no significant Internet or satellite TV penetration. The demographics are completely different. It is relatively easy for young people to emigrate. There is comparatively good and free health care and education for all. The police and military do not systematically brutalize and bloody the population. The leaders and their families are not stealing the oil wealth and openly fooling around at European casinos. You are allowed to drink, party, and have sex out of wedlock. Women are relatively liberated. There is no developed business class. The United States does not have economic relations with Cuba. Soaring wheat prices fueled the fire in lands where the poor rely on bread, while in Cuba the government has made sure that rice and beans are available for all. There have been three grassroots discussions on what ails the country over the last several years. The government has launched a significant reform of the economy, is lifting some onerous regulations on daily life, and has promised minor political reform. The Cubans cherish their hard-won social peace.

Ironically, Frank mentions but does put in as drivers the up-and-down economic situation that Cuba has endured through the years, but he and I both wonder whether Cuba could have survived without the Venezuelan influx.

When I was active in Cuba, it was going into a period where there was great economic support through a partnership with Hugo Chavez and the country of Venezuela. Cuba received cash in addition to preferentially financed oil after signing an agreement with Venezuela in 2004, which included payment for health and other technical assistance that Cuba had provided free up until that point.

Frank continues that Cuban imports totaled $6 billion in 2004 and non-tourism service income was about $1.5 billion. Just two years later, in 2006, imports nearly doubled to $10 billion and non-tourism revenue tripled to $5 billion, mainly from payments from Venezuela for medical and other technical assistance. The benefits were great with billions in joint ventures and progress. The country was not going under any time soon, as Raul Castro matriculated his power and reforms to the present day, although support from Venezuela has reduced over the years.

The Cuban government is sensitive to the population's needs through regular polling. They take a strong view of ensuring that their population has the necessary nutrients to survive and that education, culture, and medicine are provided, albeit certain medicines are short at times. I have seen hunger and poverty on the island. It's a hard living for most. Nevertheless, the Cuban people find ways to survive and rally around family despite the scarcities. Support from the US and elsewhere as supplemental transfer payments help families on the island, as does tourism, and so does the opportunity for less costly supplies that the US provides.

Cuba operated with a dual market system. Tourists and foreigners could stay at tourist hotels and use dollars to pay for goods, but the Cuban base market operated on ration books and local currency. Goods were usually scarce. There were no scarcer goods than eggs, which first went to the tourist hotels and then dollar stores. In addition to economic separation, locals were encouraged to stay away unless they directly worked with services that supported tourists and foreigners. This practice has been commonly referred to as "tourist apartheid," keep distance. The idea is that it protects sustainable tourist revenue by ensuring safety while protecting tourists from seeing poverty and substandard conditions—to keep them in the tourist bubble.[5] So, this is where we stepped into this situation, after the TSRA and after a hurricane where the US offered aid, and Castro stated that they would buy products but not accept aid.

CHAPTER TWO

Cuba Was Rocking

In 2002, Cuba was rocking. Larry Rubin, a long-time sales professional with our company, used to talk about when he sold to Cuba in the 50s: "Oh, Havana! David, if you can do anything in your life, make sure you get to Havana!" After about three hours of lines and security and being hassled in the Miami airport, I finally made it on a plane with several producers. Jim Sumner and Greg Tyler, who were in charge of USAPEEC, accompanied me. Jim Sumner is not only a great friend but also a well-known poultry industry executive and an excellent trade negotiator. He has traveled the world to negotiate trade deals and fight to eliminate restrictions. When major issues arise, Jim gets right in the thick of it. He has negotiated in instances when trade was halted and put trading companies' business in peril. He has met with US trade representatives, ambassadors, agricultural attaches around the world, and representatives from different countries.

One time, during a chicken crisis in Russia, Moscow retaliated against the chicken industry because of tariffs imposed by George W. Bush. Secretary of State Colin Powell intervened on behalf of the US poultry industry. Jim was a master of dealing with trade disasters as well as World Trade Organization rounds of negotiating on behalf of poultry and eggs. After what needed to be taken care of was done, Jim loved to go howl at the moon and have fun with the boys and girls. Meanwhile, Greg Tyler was the straitlaced guy who would eat dinner and mind the fort at home, even when on trade missions. Someone had to guard the fort at all times, and Greg made sure that the Export Council was protected.

As we got off the plane in Havana, we were escorted through security and arrived at the Hotel Nacional on the 6th executive floor, where most of the US TV networks had offices. We realized that our hotel rooms were likely bugged, but we didn't care. The Hotel Nacional is located above the Malecón, which is a roadway near Havana Harbor. In one direction, you could see the US Interests Section, which used to be the embassy.

We were quickly escorted to Alimport, which was the buying division of the foreign ministry. We were quickly surveyed by the buyers, headed by Pedro Alvarez along with Alex Perez, Ms. Yali, and Vivian Alvarez, for US business at this time. First, we were questioned about our US political contacts. I started with Andy Card, the chief of staff at the White House, Andrew Natsios, who was now heading the US Agency for International Development (USAID), and also about a dozen or more US representatives and senators from the New England delegation. These people were connections that Bill Bell, the executive director of the New England Brown Egg Council, and I routinely called on for egg industry issues. We had a decent relationship with them along with the same in Georgia, where we had a business office and the industry was very strong. These circumstances put me at the head of the class with a seat next to Fidel Castro. Pedro Alvarez was the interpreter, and he was an in-your-face, beat-on-your-price buyer and a diplomat as well.

We met with foreign diplomats in this organization. The Alimport people always seemed to be internally conflicted about doing business effectively without regulations and political red tape, not to mention having to deal with the Communist-Socialist politics. There was also a constant divorce battle in US-Cuba relations that had been manifesting over the past forty-plus years since the Cuban exiles fled to Miami and elsewhere, and certain political servants of the prior regime were executed by the new regime.

The divorce battle was deep, personal, and pitted family against family. Brothers Mario Diaz-Balart and Lincoln Diaz-Balart served in Congress from South Florida and were nephews of Fidel Castro. There are plenty of US Cubans that have family in Cuba and haven't seen them for over sixty years. The tragedy of the Cuban experience is this continued and intense adversarial divorce battle of families. The Cubans in Miami have generally prospered while the people that were left in Cuba, except for the Castro brothers, who effectively own the island, have not. Despite shortages, Cuba does an outstanding job of educating people and a decent job with health care compared to many countries in the mid and lower areas of the hemisphere.

Don't think for a moment that part of this issue is not about establishing and maintaining an economic paradise out of the land. The Cubans in Florida have built a tourist mecca in diaspora. As long as the embargo stays, they will maximize their tourism revenue and profits in Florida as US travel to the island cannot occur. I am not saying that it is all about money because it is clearly not.

The first Cuban trip I took was an introductory tour with Alimport. Later, I met with the new US Interests Section chief, Jim Cason. You always need to visit and respect the words of Professor Henry Delfiner, the token conservative on the political science faculty at Tufts University at the time I went to school there: "Reach out and learn." Jim Cason was an anti-dictator diplomat. He didn't care if they were left or right wing. He was an equal opportunity, in-your-face diplomat. In this situation, he represented the US, which was run by the Bush family, which included President George W. Bush, who effectively delegated Florida Cuban-American issues to his brother Jeb, the governor of Florida, for strategic guidance. This information was relayed to me by a person affiliated with the administration and industry. However, for Cason, he was quick to point to the failings of the Cuban regime. However, after Batista was overthrown, Cubans fled their homes and businesses, leaving them penniless in a new land. They had to start over and work hard to build a new life; he reminded us that these Cuban Americans were Americans. Further, he discussed how the Soviets supported the Cubans and kept their failed Communist system afloat as a platform against the US close to home.

Jim Cason touched on the Cuban Missile Crisis and then the Soviet's reign of tourism and integration that you still see today, with Russian Cubans that intermarried and do an outstanding job in theater and in the performing arts. Then, in the 1970s, Carter opened the Interests Section, and then through the late 1980s into the 1990s, with the Soviets on the brink, they pulled their support away from the Cubans. As noted earlier, this led the Cubans to push a double economy, one based on dollars for the foreigners and another based on pesos for Cuban citizens. It was a stark contrast with certain Cubans that do not work. For example, people that work in hotels are only allowed to be there while working. Otherwise, they are discouraged, along with the Cuban population, from interacting with foreigners. He touched on how the State Department is limited from traveling outside Havana and that they are under constant surveillance by Cuban security wherever they go.

Diplomats' homes are routinely searched, and clothes are moved from one side of the closet to the other so the diplomat knows he is being watched. Cason went into how the lack of hard currency and the failed economic system led to a negative balance of payments where Cuba was financing the economy by pushing out payments and not fulfilling the ration books that residents need to eat. Cason warned to be wary that the life you are leading down there is an image of reality. He referred to El Laguito, the section where the wealthy used to live near the Egyptian Embassy, like Russia's Potemkin village. He went on to chastise the failed Communist-Socialist dictatorship. He said that they jailed dissidents and people that speak out. They don't have one ounce of human rights or due process when they crack down and round up people. Lastly, he gave us a stern warning to be very careful, despite US law, because Cubans will screw you in the end and not pay. Perhaps not at first, but it will happen.

I asked him to reflect on why the Cuban embargo started. Here is an opportunity for US industry to get back a market of thirteen million people. They would improve the revenue to people and businesses back home. He ceded that it was the best argument we had. This trip would be one of many visits with Jim Cason. Despite our differences on the issue, he was the senior US official on the island, and I greatly appreciated his willingness to see us. Most embassies have an agriculture attaché and look to host and help us in the best possible way. Perhaps Cason will on another day. There was something extraordinary about Cason, though. He was probably one of the brightest, most well-read people that I have met. And creative as hell too! We also had the opportunity to meet Susan Archer, who was his economic head. She later left that post and was replaced by Usha Pitts, a tough-as-nails diplomat who served in Russia a year or so earlier. During this time, the honeymoon period after President Clinton left office had started to warm up relations with Cuba. The Cubans did not know what to expect.

As our visit continued, we headed out at night on a tour of Havana after dining with the guys from the chicken industry. Now I knew what Larry Rubin meant when he said I had to go to Havana someday. It was wild. Fortunately, I had my Bible and other readings. I guess I am a cross between Jim Sumner's boys and girls and Greg Tyler. Hanging out with them was a blast.

Jim Hoban was not only a great guy but also assisted us with a type of payment we had never dealt with before, which was cash against documents through a third party, like a French bank plus all the documentation. We had already applied for an Office of Foreign Assets Control (OFAC) license, which we called the "Oh-&^%$ license," to travel to Cuba. US businesses are required to attain a license from the US Department of Commerce as well. Technically, the US was still at war with Cuba, just like other rogue nations. The Cubans had no restrictions other than that they would issue you a travel visa through their interests section in Washington.

Let's get back to the great Cuban dinner that we had in Old Havana. Jim took the group to a paella place that cooked paella in a huge pan for all of us. It was culturally great, and we had a fantastic time. We were able to get Cuban cigars that outpaced anything in the States by far. The darker-grade Churchills and the lighter-grade Habanos were outstanding, and we were extremely appreciative. After we had dinner and smoked cigars, it was time for the group to split up. Generally, most of the women from the US escorted by Greg Tyler went back to the hotel, as far as we knew, and we headed off to the Old Havana Hilton, called Habana Libre.

When we got to the top of the hotel, there was a nightclub that was rocking and rolling. For guys in their thirties, forties, and fifties, it was exciting to have beautiful women meet us at the elevator and escort us to the dance floor. We weren't accustomed to this treatment. However, at this time in Cuban history, it was a relaxed environment. After a few hours, I did what I was supposed to do. I turned into a Greg Tyler and went back to my room to read the Bible. At three a.m., I heard a hard knock at the door from the chicken boys: "Hey, Radlo, how's your Bible doing?" with a noticeable laugh. "Thanks, guys. I really appreciate your kind support. Go bother Greg Tyler," I said.

My buddy John Hampton went a bit off the reservation when he got to Cuba. He had traveled with me, doing deals and helping me, for about nine years. He stayed calm and sedate and had a few beers with the boys. In any event, when it was time to go home, I'm glad I mirrored Greg Tyler and left in pretty good shape.

The next night, we went to a great restaurant on the way to Old Havana called El Chocolate in honor of a movie that was filmed in Havana. We walked up a few flights of stairs, and there were revolutionary slogans on the brick walls. We ventured to the top of the stairs, where we were escorted to an open-air restaurant that had views over the rooftops. It had the feel of the old city, and the food was fantastic.

We left El Chocolate and went directly to the old Tropicana Club. It was the place where many of Ricky Ricardo's *I Love Lucy* singing performances were based upon. I characterize it as a Latin Las Vegas before Benjamin "Bugsy" Siegel invented Vegas in the US. Everywhere you went, there were hints of what it was like in 1959 but perhaps with the old Catholic values of Fidel, who went to a Catholic school but seems to profess now to be an agnostic or an atheist. In other words, it is now PG-rated, instead of the R- or X-rated version of the Lansky-Batista era. You were allowed to smoke cigars and watch showgirls, but this was not Holland with any live X-rated features. Gambling hadn't been allowed in the country since Castro took over after Batista.

We slipped a few bucks to an employee at the Hotel Nacional who showed us where the old casino's remnants were. The Tropicana Club was still a fun and entertaining experience. Culturally, you could see the actors and actresses and the mix of Russians that participated in the shows. Cuba did an outstanding job of training artists, educating people, and putting forth literature. We were given the booklets of literature stories that were a staple for the citizenry in a school of classics. They invested in medicine and biotech, and Cuba had a leading cutting-edge industry that I will touch on later.

As we matriculated through Cuba, we appreciated the culture, the hardworking people, while observing the hard life of a Communist-Socialist system that wasn't working. I had discussions with Castro on many topics. Certainly, rewards and structure was one of them. He stared blankly at me as if he could not comprehend that financial motivation for your family was a driver and not *Socialisimo (pero muerte comprende* — but death is understandable).

During the days in Cuba, we heard ministry speeches about the revolution's gloriousness and *socialismo o muerte* (socialism or death) and how great the Communist-Socialist system was. They wanted friends for Cuba. At times, the speeches were in places where you could excuse yourself to the restroom and meet a few capitalists in the coffee area or later in the day at a bar. At night, the chicken boys were on their own, tearing up Havana.

At one point, we took a sightseeing road trip to Varadero Beach. We visited a resort that was controlled by the military. When I mean controlled by the military, I mean it was owned by Raul Castro's military, and drinks were served by guys with short-cropped hair in shorts, Caribbean shirts, and military caps. It was a paradox that I had never seen before.

On the last night, we were picked up at 7:30 p.m. and escorted to a special dinner. The bus took us to the Presidential Palace to meet with Fidel Castro. "This doesn't suck," I thought to myself. "Does not suck. Actually, pretty cool." We walked up the presidential steps, which were the same steps that Fidel and Che climbed after they forced Batista out of the country to take over the Cuban cartel.

When we arrived, they escorted us to a room in a diplomatic line. After about fifteen minutes, Fidel entered the room wearing army fatigues. He was meeting an American delegation for the first time. We assumed it had been several decades since he had met such a large group on his soil and in his palace.

It may have been the first time that he had done this here. We know he took trips to the UN, but this was Cuba, and we were an official US enemy sitting in his palace. Fidel went through the line and shook hands with everyone. He appeared to be a bit uneasy, but he was gracious. As an icebreaker, I had a book for him to sign and a gift of a Patriots hat that I had got in New Orleans at the Super Bowl a few

PHOTO 2.A. AND EXHIBIT 2.B. *The icebreaker with Castro. I suspected he wasn't a Miami Dolphins fan.*

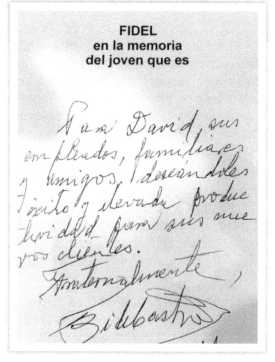

weeks earlier. I used the same offering when I met journalist Sam Donaldson at the Republican National Convention. I was an alternate delegate and floor rally coordinator when I presented Donaldson with his book to sign.

Fidel Castro finished speaking and then had some discourse with Jim Sumner. Jim sat in the middle facing him with the chairman of USAPEEC. Jim Hoban was next to him, and to Jim's left was the egg guy. I was seated next to Jim. Jim Sumner was an ever-impressive diplomat. He thanked "El

Presidente" for his graciousness and let Castro know how much the delegation had enjoyed the Cuban hospitality and ability to do business.

Next, we went to the dining room with all of the key dignitaries and the delegation. Chomi Miyar, the head of the biotech group and president of the University of Havana, attended. The secretary of the Council of State, who was Fidel's errand boy and carrier pigeon when he was in the Sierra Maestra Mountains making his guerrilla attacks on the Batista regime during the revolution, also joined Pedro Alvarez of Alimport, sitting next to him on his right. There was state security standing behind Castro at all times. Jim Sumner sat across from Castro, with Jim Hoban by his side. Alex, Ms. Yali, and Vivian from Alimport were all there, as well as Foreign Ministry officials and our entire delegation. When I found my nameplate, I realized that I was sitting next to Pedro, and I was only two seats away from Castro.

All the political advocacy over the years had paid off. Many years earlier, I had volunteered thousands of hours of my time to work for Andrew Natsios and the Republican Party. I worked with Andy Card with Natsios on President George H. W. Bush's election as well. I ran for office and worked as a floor rally delegate coordinator for the Republican National Convention and an alternate delegate with the president's sister, Nan Bush Ellis, and many others from Massachusetts. This was a very unique situation that, as noted in Principle 1 in *Principles of Cartel Disruption*, "Understand Your Opportunity and Create a Winning Value Proposition," involved politics, as it was deeply tied to Castro's "charm offensive" to attain better government relations with the United States.

For the record, my official political designation is Capitalist, and a God-believing one. However, being from Massachusetts, where most politicians were Democrats, I couldn't get one to hire me. I was interested in receiving a balanced education; I worked for Silvio Conte, a Republican, who was Tip O'Neill's best friend and was initially going to run as a Democrat. When I was in charge of the New England Brown Egg Council, I had great congressional and senatorial contacts with Republicans and Democrats and the national politicians affiliated with UEP that I supported with their political campaign contributions.

One other political contact that I recently came across was Jerry Crawford, the chairman of the Des Moines Democratic Party, which hosted every Democratic candidate to run in Iowa. He was the campaign chairman in Des Moines for Bill Clinton and Al Gore. He knew Hillary Clinton well too. We met because he was one of the attorneys who played a fixer on the legal team for Jack DeCoster. For decades, "Bad Boy" Jack found himself constantly targeted by regulators, the media, and at times the legal system for various alleged infractions. "Bad Boy" Jack always had the finest group of attorneys. He eventually ended up serving prison time due to alleged farm conditions in the state of Iowa stemming from salmonella outbreaks. I worked with Jerry on industry stuff when we needed intervention from the Clinton administration on a food safety measure. But concerning Cuba, Jerry Crawford, when I called, said, "David, I'm in. When in the US, I am Jack DeCoster's attorney. However, in Cuba, I can serve as an attorney for you."

This was great. Not only did we have the Republicans covered, but we also had the Democrats covered in a meaningful way. Also, I called Phil Olsson, our Washington counsel, and asked him to please stand by as we may need him and his contacts. I went over with Phil his connections to mesh with my contacts before I went to Cuba. By far, I had the most connections, with everyone from political advocacy work, industry work with Bill Bell in New England, nationally with UEP, Phil Olsson, and Jerry Crawford. To Fidel, I was the closest opportunity he had to have better relations with the United States. My value to him was based on who I knew.

I gave President Castro a brief background of who my close connections were. I wanted to open Cuba up to eggs. I asked Castro if there was anything he would like me to say to the White House chief of staff. And then I shut up. I didn't want to use my entire arsenal at this time. Castro responded quickly, "We are going to buy eggs." The head of the government that oversaw agriculture looked at President Castro upset. We had met with him on the trip. He was vehemently against purchasing any US eggs regardless of the supply and demand. He had the same attitude as the Cuban-Puerto Rican farmers in Puerto Rico who tried to shut us down. You will learn about that in Chapter Five of this book. However, we had Judge Pérez-Giménez in the federal judicial district of San Juan, Puerto Rico, who backed us up, and now we received an override from President Castro. We took Castro's ruling!

The agriculture secretary told us the farmers in Cuba were Castro's base for the revolution. Besides our differences with the agriculture secretary and the farmers, we had a good discussion about agriculture, including feed costs, diseases, food distribution, and refrigeration, or lack thereof.

Eggs that were exported from the United States had quality specifications that included refrigeration requirements and USDA certification that were required to ship to Cuba. These specifications were similar to those in Puerto Rico, where I had done business previously. There were two standards like Puerto Rico, refrigeration and USDA quality for US eggs, and no quality standards and no refrigeration for Cuban eggs. The Cuban agricultural leader thought it would be better to discuss the issue on another occasion with Fidel and not cause disruption to the diplomatic mission of Cuba for that night.

Castro agreed to buy US eggs. Pedro looked at me and said, "We have a deal, my friend." We quickly finished the details of price and volume while Castro answered a question with a forty-five-minute answer. Before Castro was done, we smoked cigars to celebrate the sealed deal. That night we dined on salad and lobster tails and finished with a great Café Cubano.

What do you do when you get one order? You shut up for a while and wait for the opportunity to get another one! After Castro was done, he had a sidebar with me about US politics, with Pedro interpreting in broken English. This was fortunate because, after a week of listening to Spanish, I began to recall the language from my schooling and from when I did business in Puerto Rico. It was helpful to hear Castro's question or statement in Spanish and then hear it in English.

I wasn't intimidated by Fidel Castro, despite his uniform and the security guards with machine guns. As my dad said, "Any politician is a man that puts one pant leg on at a time." Fidel was a master politician that outlived many US presidents and administrations that hoped for his demise, along with the CIA that sought to assassinate him but failed. He was the de facto king of Cuba, and he basically owned the country with his brother and his family while running the former cartel that is now effectively owned by the Castros and their regime.

PHOTO 2C: *At the end of the night, while the others in the delegation were getting autographs, I smoked a Cuban cigar for breaking into Cuba with business on two separate business deals and the start of unofficial discussions.*

Fidel spoke about PPG, which was a sugar pill that was claimed to lower cholesterol. I saw this as an opportunity to ask Fidel and Chomi if I could have the chance to import the technology and commercialize it if we got proper licensing. Fidel said, "Done." Chomi looked at me not like the ag secretary but with a surprised look. I then put a cigar in my mouth and started to puff on it. The business was done. I had some minor conversations with Fidel and got a picture between Fidel and Pedro with a cigar. I donated the photograph to the Tufts University Athletics Department to be viewed near the trophy case because I did not want my son, Ben, to see me smoking. Chomi thought that was hilarious. I then went back to my seat and finished the cigar while the rest of the delegation swarmed Fidel for autographs.

On the first night, I established a relationship with Fidel Castro, Pedro Alvarez, and Chomi Miyar, which later led me to an introduction to Carlos Borrotto, a key executive in ag biotech. The orders I received helped to pay for the trip, and we broke back into Cuba on behalf of the entire US egg industry and fellow poultrymen and farm businessmen.

After dinner, we had a group picture in front of the palace. On this night, we stayed at the Hotel Nacional and sat outside on the veranda looking out at the cannons of the USS *Maine*, which was sunk over a century ago in Havana Harbor. We smoked cigars and drank Cuban mojitos and *siete anos* Havana Club rum with ice. We gave up howling at the moon that night to have drinks with Greg Tyler, Jim Hoban, Jim Sumner, and the boys and girls. It was an excellent finish to a memorable night. USAPEEC trade missions were exciting incremental revenue opportunities, and regulars also usually included Jean Murphy of USAPEEC, Mark Barrett of Lamex, Chaz Wilson, and Thierry Murad of AJC.

That night, I think even the Tyson guys stayed on the veranda, for a while at least. The poultry-related traders and producers like Keith Steinberg of Waltkoch; Jim Hoban, Larry Lieberman, and Bob Breyan of Boston Agrex; my buddy Suj Niyangoda, David Hand, and Jim Wayt, along with partners; John along with Jim Baker; the boys and girls from the big prestigious brokerage firm, AJC; and Sanderson Farms, Pilgrim's Pride, Perdue, and Tyson all walked away with some significant orders. John Joyner of Dolphin Shipping also benefited directly from my discussions with Fidel Castro. It was one hell of a trade mission. I bought Jim Sumner a ton of drinks that night. He then referred to me as "Daveed," as Castro called me, and he did for the next several years during a slew of meetings and fun times we had.

In between discussions with Fidel, I kept notes of his main points for the local and national press. Here are some of the highlights that ended up in multiple press articles locally and nationally:

1. "We have a higher literacy rate than most of the world, and most Cubans can speak English, Spanish, and another language."

2. "We have a tremendous arts program that is unparalleled in the world."

3. "You Americans are competition addicted."

4. "If there was bilateral trade, you would get half of the agriculture imports with a growth from $35 million to $500 million."

5. "American people have more money than they can spend in their life."

6. "The embargo is causing the poor, the middle class, and the elderly to go without proper nutrition. Cuba is paying 15–20% more by not being able to buy from the United States."

7. "You trade with Vietnam, where you had fifty thousand citizens die, and trade with China, where you have differences. Why don't you trade with us?"

8. "We are committed to the War on Terror with the United States."

9. "We have to import grains because of the climate. If the world had a drought, we would die. If China had a drought, it would deplete the world food supply."

10. "We are going to buy eggs from your industry." "Radlo will get the opportunity, based upon securing appropriate licenses to import PPG, other drugs, and intellectual property and technologies."

Back in the States

When we got back to the States, I was delighted to bring a couple of boxes of cigars to my retail customers who had requested them. Without naming names, Hannaford, Stop & Shop, Roche Bros., Caribbean Produce, Central Produce, Market Basket, and some great employees received cigars. On the first day back, I went outside and smoked a cigar with Valerie Vastis, our Specialty Customer Service Orders employee, aka the Egg Lady, at Radlo Foods (Born Free and Eggland's Best). Valerie was great at putting out fires for us. She could also make old, dry cigars fresh. I made sure Valerie had a few Cubans to take home.

Valerie was the main person in the office who paid the price because my Innermetrix found a blind spot of not empathizing when I was stressed, as found in Principle 5 in *Principles of Cartel Disruption*: "Clearly Understand and Utilize People Resources." Fortunately, when that happened, I had a process to have Stephanie Norton, our VP of HR and Admin., close my door, bring Valerie into her office, and calm her down. The following day, when I felt calm, my empathy returned.

I would apologize to Valerie for being short and abrupt. At that point, I could listen to the issues and how she solved them. However, when it was a horrible day, or, on this occasion, coming back from a great experience, I would go down and smoke with Valerie and, at times, John Stevens, outside. They were real smokers.

I mostly like to chew on cigars. I learned that from the founder of Cal-Maine Foods, Fred Adams. His son-in-law Dolph, a great politician, ended up taking over as president and now chairman. He oversaw the significant rise of Cal-Maine along with Ken Looper. I saved a few cigars for Fred, some other partners, suppliers, and customers.

My friend "Ole Southern Boy John," as they say down South, as noted earlier, had a rough spell in Cuba and came back to the states ill. He had done some hooting and hollering with the boys and girls from the industry. Going to bed early and reading the Bible, as noted, paid dividends to me. John stayed on my board and handled real estate, which pleased everyone involved.

At home, my kids were delighted to see me, and I got back to reality. We gave a scoop to the Lewiston *Sun Journal* in Auburn, Maine, about the trip in copious detail and how brown eggs from Maine made it to Cuba. It was a front-page lead. The *Portland* (Maine) *Press Herald* ran a similar story, as did, believe it or not, the *Miami Herald*.

In the New Hampshire papers, there was a story about Pete and Gerry's New Hampshire Organic Eggs. We sold them under the Born Free brand to Castro. We also had a story published that helped flip a US politician on Cuba issues relative to lifting travel restrictions. The *Portland Press Herald* and *Boston Globe* followed, and so did AP. We had NBC and ABC following us in Maine, as well as the local news stations. It was a great national story.

I will never forget Mark Halperin, who was at ABC at the time and looking for a golden sound bite. I gave it to him in ten seconds on the first try. He said to the producer, "Turn off the camera and recorder. I need to ask something." Then Halperin said, "Are you really an egg farmer? You sound like you are a professional." I didn't explain that I had turned down government jobs to be an egg man. I told him I had heard that the press can make or destroy a business in a twenty-four hour news cycle. I asked him if he were in my shoes, would he make it a priority to communicate to the media and the general public effectively? That shut Halperin right up. He got a few more sound bites and told the producer he had what he needed. It aired that night on ABC News. It was a fun time to be able to connect with the media in a non-damage-control manner. Good stories built our reputation nationally in the industry. It was also positive for the community, sustainable leadership, and our brands.

The local print, radio, and television media did several stories on the Cuban venture. NBC did several stories on Cuba. We sincerely appreciated Mary Murray, the NBC bureau chief in Havana, who objectively reported the great strides in new economic activity with the US food and agriculture industry. We were featured later in several spots on NBC News that focused on Cuba and the embargo. The contract footage with Castro became B-roll for NBC demonstrating that US business was back for several years.

Our news created a positive force to help US farmers by doing business in Cuba. Our congressman and senators were supportive of us with this new economic activity and were more inclined to support the easing of trade and travel restrictions between the US and Cuba. The Cuban cartel appreciated the positive media. We received millions of positive media impressions for our brands Eggland's Best and Born Free, which raised the stature of Radlo Foods.

Turning the Charm Offensive into Real Sustainable Business

At the same time, I reached out to Bill Bell, the New England Brown Egg Council's executive director. Bill was an Ivy League guy who worked at the State Department many years before in Curaçao. He had substantial connections, especially in the state of Maine. I asked Bill whether he could arrange with

John Nutting, the chairman of the Maine Senate's ag committee, to cosponsor legislation calling for an end to the embargo. John was a Democrat and a dairy farmer that neighbored our Leeds, Maine, operation.

I asked him to check with the potato boys and girls from Aroostook County concerning the Republicans' joint agriculture committee. I promised them a trip to Havana to meet Fidel Castro if they could pull this off. Bill told me he thought it would be cool to go to Havana, meet with Fidel, and see the culture and the history. I told him I would set it up as soon as we got the resolution. Bill put a resolution together in collaboration with Senator Nutting. They worked it through the system and eventually got a vote to the floor that was debated seriously and passed. As promised, John Nutting, State Veterinarian Don Hoenig, Bill Bell, and many others came to Cuba. Eventually, Governor John Baldacci, who was a great supporter of agriculture, came down too.

When we went down the next time, we were met at the Foreign Ministry

PHOTO 2.D. *Pictured below at the head of the table is Chomi Miyar, who was Fidel's errand boy from the revolution. He was the chancellor of the University of Havana, secretary to the Council of States, and head of the biotech industry. Chomi made fun of me hanging with Fidel with a cigar coming out of my mouth. Also pictured opposite me is Carlos Borroto, who was the head of ag-biotech. Across the table from me is Phil and Pedro. Yali is beside me.*

plane and quickly whisked out through the tarmac's side door. We were brought to a protocol house with an elegant pool across from the Egyptian Embassy.

During that trip, I wanted to continue the business relationship and commence discussions with biotech and PPG groups. When I met Castro for the first time privately, the conversation focused heavily on farming and business. He was a passionate advocate of agribusiness. We had a long discussion about everything: poultry, eggs, feed, food distribution, nutrition, health, wellness, and medical care. It was an enlightening discussion. Castro drilled down into my cost structure and started to discuss the components that made up the food that the animals were eating to lower the feed cost. In great detail, he discussed how the Soviets had brought cows that were very productive for colder Russian conditions but could not produce well in warmer climates. He made it clear that agriculture was an important issue and passion of his, and we could not pull any shenanigans with him.

Then Castro turned to me and said, "Daveed, you have been around our country now on two trips. My brother and I own this island. He runs the business and military, and I run the politics. What do you think of our costs?" *Holy sh-t*, I thought. He did have an economic system. He based his economic system on earning cash, staying in power, sustainably educating the masses, providing health care and enough food based on the people's life expectancy, and working hard for the causes expressed by his driven nationalism. He said that elections were an absolute waste of money. Instead, he wanted to use the money to feed the poor and the world. He believed that the money for elections was wasted on the media. This usage did not advance anything but media ratings. It came very quickly that Fidel was a king, but he was a king with some noble intentions that allowed him to stay in power for as long as he had.

The Bush administration played both sides of the coin with the Cuban-American exiles to please the boys and girls of America's economics. Later, President Obama installed a formal ambassador in Cuba instead of an Interests Section chief. Secretary of State John Kerry of Massachusetts also supported this installation.

Castro said that our system was dysfunctional and not serving the people. He was also concerned with the rise of feed cost globally, driven by the US using food for fuel, such as ethanol. He believed in sustainable causes of zero poverty, reduced hunger, education, and sustainable food systems but drew the line at having sustainability cost the poor more. He wasn't worried about cheaper goods arriving at his shores. He was content to have his population do other productive things. He said perhaps they would participate more in the arts, teach, coach, or do something else to aid society.

We then spoke in detail about the senators, congressional members, and my other contacts in the administration. I shared more of my contacts that

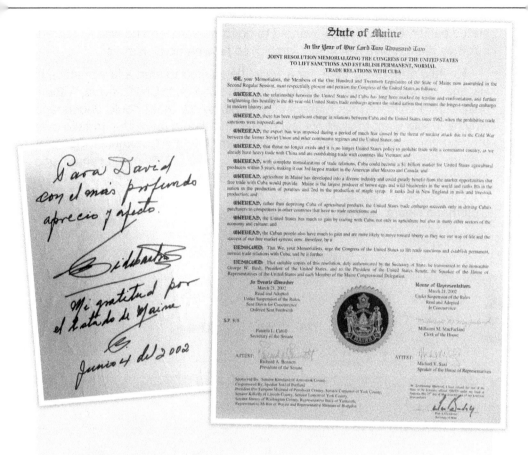

EXHIBIT 2E1 AND 2E2. *June 4, 2002, I presented Fidel Castro's proclamation from the state of Maine.*

I had not mentioned when we first met. I believed strongly that farm-state Republicans and the New England delegation would respond well to the opportunity to do more business with Cuba, especially when it affected their constituents. I promised that I would be back after I had a chance to meet with the folks in Washington. I left Cuba with additional signed orders. It was another productive trip. I then set my sights on getting to Washington to meet with the people I knew.

After a productive meeting with Phil Olsson, my Washington, DC, legal counsel and senior partner of OFW Law, I gave Castro the resolution, and he was thrilled. I had never seen him so inspired. He turned to me and spoke English for the first and only time. He said, "I am a very happy and pleased man." He reminisced about Columbia and living on the Upper West Side of a third-floor apartment. He said it was one of the happiest times of his life. As I stated earlier, Castro initially wanted to go to Harvard, and he was accepted, but they did not give him a scholarship, so he went to Columbia.

He said after being there for a while, he wanted to start a law practice in Havana. He had aspirations to later begin a revolution with Che Guevara. Without hesitation, I validated his reasoning. I let him know that I could understand why he would want to start his law career and then a revolution to take over the country. In that way, you could transform it into a Communist-Socialist system with low-cost health care and literacy for all, 100% market share, and own the Cuban cartel with your family. "*Si, El Presidente*, I get it," I told him. I did not know what else I could say at that time. He kindly gave the group diplomatic cigars, and he gave me his business card.

CHAPTER THREE:

Incubation to Acceleration of Sustainable US Industry Business in Cuba—Delivering an Outstanding Value Proposition while Working to Transform for a Safer, New, and Better World

Map Marketing

When I got back from the trip, I contacted Ron Mills, my political consultant from my state representative days. He was Christine Bushway's partner at the time. She was a Radlo Foods board member. I shared an idea with Ron and asked him to poke holes in it. I suggested we create a map of the agricultural commodities, starting with eggs, and expand from there to pinpoint all of them. Then we'd record on the map who supports ending the embargo, who is against ending the embargo, and who is undecided or new. I suggested we then follow the same process for ending travel restrictions to Cuba.

Together, we created the initial map for the next trip to Cuba, but Mills came back with a blockbuster idea. He said that he had a friend at the Republican National Committee that could get him a map that listed the votes for Bush and Gore on the RNC map as a backdrop for what we were planning to do. Ron hit it out of the park! Then he said, "And Castro will have the voter tally from the new numbers produced before the Democratic National Committee right after the elections if we want to wait or do a follow-up map."

Ron went down to his war room and made the maps. They were unbelievable.

Christine Bushway said that she couldn't even get him on the phone because he was so committed to the project. When he finished the maps, I drove to his home in New Hampshire. I thought they were fabulous. I told him how grateful I was and also thought we were going to do well with them. I had never seen Ron so proud. I knew it would take our relationship with Fidel Castro and the Cubans to a new level while maintaining our US government relationships.

The maps clearly outlined a huge value proposition to Fidel Castro. As noted, I discuss the value proposition in the first principle found in Chapter One of *Principles of Cartel Disruption*. They could see visually the opportunity of what congressional and senatorial districts they could buy from and also see those that were undecided or against Cuba trade and travel restrictions. The map allowed me to teach Fidel Castro how politics flows from economics in United States democracy. It starts with economic interests that are improved by business with Cuba. In these situations, politicians generally back local business and industry.

With Cuba, it was not just about getting the best products at the cheapest price. This opportunity was an additional value proposition that we brought to the table by selling to Cuba. Local politicians were persuaded in some instances to support lifting the trade embargo and travel restrictions. Some will say, "But David, if you removed the embargo, you wouldn't be selling cash up front that ensures payment." That is correct, but this exercise was about showing incremental progress of increased support with the end goal of attaining great long-term sustainable business through a value proposition that had a competitive advantage. We were well aware that Cuban-American interest groups back home would be advocating in the other direction that would keep the embargo intact for a long time and our cash-up-front situation stabilized. Likewise, in Cuba, some have argued that rallying against the embargo was the common theme that sustained Fidel Castro in power for multiple decades. The "common enemy approach" effectively promoted nationalism in Cuba. It's like social progressives in the US at times pushing for Socialism. Do they really want the US to end up as a Socialist-Communist system like Cuba? I encourage you to please go down and visit and review their economic and social situation and decide for yourself.

Ron passed away during the Cuban years. We had a service at the Old North Church in Boston. I spoke and said that if Ron Mills was around during the revolution that started in 1775, there would have been many more options than "one if by land or two if by sea," referencing the two lanterns that were eventually hung at the top of the Old North Church signaling the British Army's venturing out of Boston by sea.

I could only imagine the maps that Ron Mills would have drawn to assist Sam Adams with the revolution. Ron was one of the best creative political minds that I knew. I miss him to this day. Peter Blute, a former congressman who worked with Ron, came to the funeral. Later, Peter became a broadcaster and accompanied me on a Cuba trip with NBC affiliate WBZ News' Robin Hamilton.

Andy and Andrew

The next thing that I did was contact Andy Card, the current White House chief of staff who worked for the H. W. Bush campaign. Early on, Andy told me that it would be challenging to get to him by sending correspondence or calling the White House. He told me it was better to send a copy to his home. I had his address from years earlier, so I sent it there in hopes that he was still residing there or that it would forward to his new address.

I wanted to meet with him or someone who could help me attain the biotech product licenses and expand the Cuban business. I needed someone I could pass on information that I received from Castro. I believed that it was important to the White House for a few reasons. The first was that I thought there was an honest dialogue going with a wave of support from states and districts that were getting business from Cuba along with many more that would benefit from increased business with them. This relationship was not only a regional issue but a national issue.

George W. Bush made a campaign promise to Cuba, but he had not yet unleashed any policy statements on the subject. We saw it as an opening to lobby like hell in food and agriculture. The media attention to this issue was a positive factor. John Bolton from the State Department warned that there might be weapons of mass destruction or other harmful weapons that Cuba was housing. This timeframe led up to the Iraq War, when the US was reeling after 9/11, creating heightened concern. I wanted to help, given my new access to Cuba's Communist dictator and known enemy of the United States.

Andrew Natsios, my former boss when he was Republican state chair in Massachusetts and state representative, quickly got back to me and said the next time that I was in town to give him a call. I had seen Andrew through the years and was grateful to continue the relationship with him.

Then, the CIA called. They had seen the press reports and knew that I was in Cuba and had had direct conversations with Castro and his power structure. *They are always listening*, I thought. I called Phil Olsson in Washington. After consultation with Phil, I called the CIA representative back and told the person that Radlo Foods would be willing to meet in Phil Olsson's law office in the conference room. They agreed, so I made an appointment to go to Washington within a week.

At the same time, I received communication from the White House. Andy Card had Colonel Emilio Gonzalez, the director of National Security for Western Hemisphere Affairs, contact me. He was a straightforward guy who arranged a White House meeting with me in his office. He held the same position as Colonel Oliver North from the Reagan administration.

When I got down to Washington, I had a full schedule. Phil Olsson prepped me to meet with the CIA, and I met with Andrew, who was in charge of USAID. The CIA meeting lasted about two hours. Most of the CIA's discussions must be kept confidential, but I think it is appropriate to share one specific agenda item. They questioned me about the potential for Cuban bioweapons and weapons of mass destruction.

Over the next several months and years, I continued to confirm two important items in conversations with Castro, others in the biotechnology group, and the foreign ministry. This assertion made it to the press on May 6, 2002. It came from John Bolton, who was undersecretary for Arms Control and

Disarmament at that time in the State Department. He has served in numerous positions since then, including national security advisor to President Trump. He is a bright, prestigious man, and his comments heed concern.

According to a CNN news piece, Bolton, through an address to the Heritage Foundation, demanded that Cuba stop sharing biological weapons technology with nations unfriendly to the United States. "Cuba has provided dual-use biotechnology to other rogue states," Bolton said. "We are concerned that such technology could support biological warfare programs in those states." Bolton called on Cuba to "cease all biological weapons cooperation with rogue states and to fully comply with all obligations under the Biological Weapons Convention."

Cuba was one of the seven countries that the State Department considered state sponsors of terror. Bolton continued that Cuba not only had a role in spreading weapons technology but also was a longtime human rights violator that provided a haven for terrorists. He said Cuba's role is underplayed in threatening US security.

The Cubans categorically denied having bioweapons. Further, they agreed to regular independent third-party inspections of biotech facilities. The Cubans directly addressed this issue. From what I could uncover, the worst situation that the Cubans might have had was toxic waste similar to our toxic waste sites in the US. The other issue was that they needed multiparty corroboration and worked hard to help them access said corroboration. In the words of President Ronald Reagan, "Trust, but verify." This means that Cuba would be assured that there would not be Cuban-American politics fused into the inspections to make them unfair that they were concerned about.

After 9/11, many US government capabilities were in the process of being upgraded, including the gathering of intelligence on serious issues. The CIA was very straightforward in telling me that they would take any information that I had now. They told me that because I was a US resident, I should cooperate with them based on patriotism, and they would never pay any expenses or compensation. Frankly, I never asked them for either, as it was an incumbent giveback program to help our country.

They were looking for validation of other items but nothing that rose to the importance of bioweapons. It was their mission to report to Congress along with the executive branch. They took their unbiased political viewpoints very seriously and worked hard to deliver selfless patriotism devoid of partisan rancor. I know that they were likely taking flack from the administration and the State Department for not toeing the administration's line. Still, they saw a higher calling in delivering intelligence. The most exciting part of dealing with the US government in Cuba was watching the inter-bureau and -branch rivalry between the State Department, the CIA, the White House, and Congress.

When I met in Phil's office afterward, I noticed that they asked questions that revealed they didn't have a robust intelligence platform for gathering information due to budgetary and legal constraints. It concerned me about other rogue nations. I asked them if they had the same level of intelligence in the Middle East. They said they were working on training more agents and were short of people who spoke Farsi. Due to US legal restrictions, they were not allowed to pay US residents for information, only foreigners. Then I said, "Just like you don't have that many agents in Cuba that can verify information on bioweapons."

When the US agents went to Cuba, they were under the same restrictions as State Department personnel on travel. Cuban diplomats were in Washington's Interests Section and the United Nations. Meanwhile, not only could I travel throughout the country at any time, but I had the option to have a driver shuttle me around if I desired. Showing a picture of Castro and me permitted me to operate freely in the country; people would get nervous and let me pass. I had Castro's blessing to go anywhere I wished.

I think people have been too tough on the CIA during this period. They were operating under rules of intelligence put forth by Congress, which frankly did not allow US residents to be paid. With limited access to rogue nations, it wasn't easy to get intelligence from these countries. From what I've observed, the CIA and Congress have worked in good faith to resolve these issues after 9/11.

I met with Colonel Emilio Gonzalez at the White House and developed a good working relationship with him over time. Based on our discussions, I gleaned the tactical issues connected to his strategy with Cuba. The overall strategy was a function of the White House. I came in as an industry guy that was economically doing business and expanding our portfolio.

The White House gave our industry support worldwide and looked to have a favorable business climate with decreased regulations and taxes. It was new to have industry back in Cuba. We had positive press behind us and purchase orders for America. At the same time, the White House was heavily weighing the interests of the Cuban-American community, which was supportive of the current administration as well as Governor Bush in Florida. I explained to Colonel Gonzalez that there was an excellent opportunity to help Americans and US industry with products shipped there. Also, there was an opportunity to have lifesaving drugs.

I agreed with the colonel that we did appreciate getting paid in cash and that some credit issues were substantial given our country's problems with Cuba and their economy. Still, the overall opportunity was not *chicken feed*. This opportunity had the potential for billions in revenue for US industry. He seemed to back off a bit, and sounded a bit like some senior members in the administration as he said, "You boys and girls can go down there and have all the dinners you want and get all the business you want." We are not standing in your way of US law.

In the first meeting, he suggested that there was consideration for US farm tractors to be shipped and added to the TSRA that allowed both food and medicine to reach Cuba. He punted to OFAC regarding getting licenses to import additional technology. OFAC could shut anyone down at any time, and it was a branch of government as part of the Treasury that you did not take lightly.

I asked him to continue dialogue based upon overtures from Castro about future discussions on US relations. On the first visit, Colonel Gonzalez did not shut the door. I interpreted this as a signal that the higher-ups in the administration were reviewing the matter or discussing it among themselves. We started a conversation with many farm-state Republicans in Congress that were getting business. They were quite enthused with the discussion, and it was all positive in the media about Cuba at this time. I told the colonel that the CIA had contacted me, and I continued to work in good faith with them.

I knew Cuban-American Otto Reich, who was staunchly anti-Castro and Cuba, was in the State Department, and so was right-winger Dan Fisk, who I believed worked with Senator Jesse Helms. They were an anti-Cuba group. John Bolton was also the head of Arms Control and Disarmament. Otto Reich was not a big fan of businessmen going to Cuba or contacting the Cuban regime. Together, these men were the most neoconservative and were steadfastly against the expansion of further business with the Cuban regime. They advocated less contact and more isolation in diplomatic relations. Our industry pushed for constructive engagement and other openings of relations to maximize economic development with Cuba.

Next, I went to USAID and met with Andrew Natsios. It was a casual meeting. Andrew was efficient and bright. He was eager to show me his office and meet the people in USAID, who did excellent work. Andrew apologized for being a few minutes late after coming from the White House. President Bush wanted to discuss additional aid for Africa as part of his compassionate conservatism agenda. I knew how much Andrew had worked in Africa over the years. He was the special envoy to Darfur to stop ethnic cleansing, and bullets hit his car during his years of service. Fortunately, he was not injured.

There are not enough men like Andrew Natsios. I have great respect for him, and he was a great mentor. He has a photographic memory, which was helpful when he testified before a committee. He arrived to work early and stayed late. He was also a reserve officer in the military. He was humble, a moderate conservative in both values and treasure. When I ran for office, he cautioned me about choosing not to support unions on prevailing wages. He was right but relented when I showed my passion for not supporting it, even though it was a factor in my election loss.

After many years of working with unions, in retrospect, I should have reconsidered the issue and the value that police and fire bring to local communities. I based my view on a recent union vote in our family's small business that would have ended the company.

After we had our meeting and he was open to Cuba, he put me in touch with several others at USAID to understand their programs' breadth. All the people I spoke with that day praised Andrew as the best administrator of USAID and wished he would stay forever. These were all civil servants that worked in both Republican and Democratic administrations.

I left USAID and went to Capitol Hill to meet with several congressional and senatorial offices and then headed back to Phil Olsson's office to debrief the meetings. When I got home, I called my travel agent to book Cuba trips.

El Mappe

Back home, I contacted Pedro and Castro's office to let them know that I met with Washington and would return to Havana shortly. Phil Olsson accompanied me on this trip. When we exited the airplane, Alex Perez met us in a black Mercedes with a driver. We got our baggage and left through the back door on the tarmac. Pedro took our passports and had them appropriately stamped.

After we got settled, we met with Pedro and Alex at the Hotel Nacional. I brought the map to show Alex, and he was impressed. Then, we had a quick meeting at Alimport. Pedro entered the meeting room and said excitedly, "*Donde esta* El Mappe?" I showed it to him. He smiled and looked at me slowly. "Okay," he said. "Now we are in business. Now Daveed, please explain this." I explained the dots' representation on the map. It showed every congressional and senatorial district in America superimposed with the votes from the presidential election. Then I showed him the votes that would eliminate the embargo and travel restrictions to Cuba. I went through the areas that had the best opportunity to acquire products from congressional districts undecided on travel and trade restrictions or that were against them but may change if there was increased economic activity from Cuba purchases from in-district businesses.

"Well, Daveed, if the prices from these areas are the same, we will buy," Pedro said. I turned to the right as an assistant came into the room. He let Pedro know that Fidel was on the phone for him. He immediately excused himself and came back about forty-five minutes later. He said that Fidel was looking forward to meeting with me a couple of days after concluding the business. It was getting late, so we were driven back to the house where we were staying.

The next day we had a meeting at the biotech plaza to see Carlos Borroto. He was a worldwide expert on ag-biotech. Chomi let him know that we would come, and he was ready with a complete dog and pony show. We were astonished by the medicine and agri-biotech projects the Cubans were involved with, including medical devices, medical drugs, orphan drugs, tilapia farming, and many other medical and ag-biotech areas. I had experience with world-class doctors and researchers at Vicam with the biotech partnership in Watertown, Mass., with the best research minds in their fields. I had the privilege to work with Dr. Livingston and Dr. Benjamin from Harvard, Dana Farber, Dr. Wogan, Dr. Tannenbaum, and Dr. Cohn from MIT, Dr. Groopman from Johns Hopkins, and others. Carlos Borroto was known in Cuba and worldwide to be one of the brightest and most engaging minds and agriculture-biotechnology executives in the field. He was fantastic when it came to ag-biotech, presenting, and research. He was electric and spent many years working for the United Nations overseas.

After the presentation, we met with the sugar pill PPG makers. The product was proclaimed to reduce cholesterol naturally. The clinical name was Cuban Policosanol. Phil Olsson and I were impressed with their science on the subject. The head of Dalmer Labs gave us the history of the revolution and boasted about how much Fidel had given to Cuba. He was thankful that Fidel came to power and had fantastically run Cuba for all of these years. Phil and I were politically correct and thanked him for sharing his thoughts.

We spoke about our interest in taking the drug to OFAC, which regulated financial commerce in the US, and petitioning to export the intellectual property to the US. Castro was excited about the potential of doing so. He smiled and said, "I know. I heard." We had the deal. We still needed their official sign-off and needed their lawyer to draft some language with Phil. That was taken care of on a subsequent trip. We were going to push this up the flagpole while we planned to work with the Center for Genetic Engineering and Biotechnology (CIGB) on one drug. That's probably the best that we could ask for at the time. Phil Olsson was going to petition the appropriate authorities for permission in Washington to import intellectual property to the US. We intended to import an orphan drug medical technology as well with Borroto's colleagues at the CBIC.

We then were taken back to our house, and we jumped in the pool midafternoon. We turned to each other, and I said to Phil, "At Harvard, how do you say this does not suck?" Without hesitation, in his lawyerly Ivy League voice, Phil said, "This is pretty great, David. Indeed, this does not suck." He puffed on a Habanos cigar, and we enjoyed some banter.

That night after a mojito at one of Hemingway's favorite bars, La Bodeguita del Medio, we chose to have dinner in Old Havana at a restaurant near the square. As we walked after dinner, Phil noticed an older cigar salesman wearing a Jewish kippah. Phil is about six foot three and was able to spot him easier than me at five ten.

We stopped, and he offered us cigars. We gladly received them. Then, with his kippah on, I asked the man whether he could give us a tour of the Jewish section in Old Havana and teach us some of the history of the Jews in Cuba. He was thrilled to oblige our request. He said his name was Luis Sklarz, and he was a retired foreign services agent that oversaw nickel trading with London and other cities.

Very quickly, he gave us a bird's-eye view of the Cuban economy. Here was a bright, retired, older Cuban that did decades of service as a senior officer for the Cuban government, both as we later came to know it diplomatically and economically, as well as intelligence services. He was selling cigars in the street. Phil and I looked at each other incredulously.

Luis did an impeccable job of giving us a tour of Old Havana, including a visit to his shul, where he prays every day in a minion in the morning. He was traditionally Jewish, if not Orthodox, and did everything he could to keep kosher. He had family that moved to the United States, and he had not communicated with them since before the revolution. Because of the deterioration of relations between the countries and his loyalty to Cuba, a breakup was inevitable.

Also, Luis gave a compelling one-hour rendition of the Jewish migration to Cuba and a discussion of excommunicated Jews in Spain who arrived as Catholics. That may explain the similarities between the Jewish people and Cubans, but it is still up for much debate. He even said that he wrote a book about the topic.

To say that we adopted Luis and brought him into the family is an understatement. Luis ended up servicing the entire US agriculture industry with cigars. We told Luis to meet us the next day at the Nacional, where he would deliver us some Habanos. As we were having the conversation, state security approached Luis and told him not to speak with foreigners. Luis left and headed to the temple.

The following day, I met with Alex and Pedro in the morning and talked through the details of the future egg shipments. We were delighted with the business, as was the US egg industry. We were also pleased that they gave many of our agriculture friends orders. Over the years, we got to know the cream of the crop of agriculture over trade missions and cocktail parties in Cuba.

To give you some context of who was over there doing business that I was working with, here is a brief list: my future board member Tony DeLio, president of the nutraceuticals division of ADM; Marvin Lehrer of the USA Rice Federation; members of the poultry and egg industry, including but not limited to Don DeLordo of Michigan Turkey; David Hand of Pilgrim's Pride; Larry Lieberman, Bob Breyan, and Suj Niyangoda of Boston Agrex; Keith Steinberg from Waltkoch; Ernesto Baron, Jim Sumner, and Greg Tyler of the Export Council; John Joyner of Dolphin Shipping; Eric Joiner of AJC, who had a few of his folks down; Jim Hoban, who was the USAPEEC chair at the time;

a rash of others from Tyson, Perdue, and Gold Kist; and assorted friends and family from the chicken, turkey, duck, and egg world.

We discussed some logistics on shipping and called back home to speak with our export division, Jim Corbin and Nicky McKinney, out of Gainesville, GA. All was in order, and we were moving forward to ship with a signed agreement. When business was complete, an appointment was scheduled for us at 2:00 p.m., although we weren't told with whom. At 1:45 pm, the car pulled up and brought us to the Palco Convention Center. We entered a side door, and then Fidel drove up in his motorcade. He got out of his car to greet us. We went upstairs in the elevator with state security to his offices. They escorted us to a room that looked like a lock-safe bunker for our meeting. He had the same woman, who I learned later was the mother of one of Fidel's children, Juanita Vera, translating. They had impeccable chemistry together, and I enjoyed meeting with them both. Pedro was at the meeting, and we all had a tremendous initial conversation.

Then, Fidel wanted to break out some great wine that he had received as a gift from a diplomat from Spain. As we were drinking the wine, Pedro gave the introduction to the map in Spanish. Fidel said through his interpreter, "So, Daveed, you have something to show us?" Fidel was always a lawyer at heart. I said, "Yes, Mr. President, I do. Please let me take this out." I unrolled the map and placed it on the coffee table in front of where we were meeting. I got down on one knee in front of him and started explaining all of the map information. I went through every state in the union and explained what type of agricultural commodities could be purchased. For example, I said we were buying products from ME, FL, NH, OH, PA, FL, GA, SC, NC, and IA. The chicken came from AR and VA. The turkey came from SC and MI. Also, there were opportunities to buy salmon from AK and maple syrup from VT. "When you buy from us, we take working the map seriously," I said. As a reminder, always close the sale with the value proposition to address the pain point and shut up!

Castro was taken aback at first, and then he kneeled across from me, raised his hand, and slammed his finger down in the middle of Pennsylvania. "Gettysburg!" he exclaimed. "The Confederacy made a big mistake taking on the Union Army fighting uphill. That's what lost them the battle. When I was in the Sierra Maestra Mountains, attacking down and coming back, we had the advantage because we had the high ground. I learned that from Gettysburg!" he boasted.

He went on for about twenty minutes, continuing to kneel right in front of me, on the war tactics used in the battles of the Civil War, and then in great detail on the battles against Batista's forces that brought him to Havana in victory. He went back to the landing of his ship, the *Granma*, the fights that they had to get into the Sierra Maestra Mountains, and how the farmers were there to support him all along the way.

I realized that he started to posture for business negotiation. He continued his discussion about talks he had had with Che Guevara, his brother Raul, how his errand boy Chomi Miyar ferried packages, and how Gustavo Machín's dad heroically died in the war, shedding blood so that Socialism and Communism would prevail. Fidel was a few inches away from me at this time, raising his hand and gesturing about the memories like it was yesterday.

After about an hour of this, he went back into his chair. He said, "Okay, Radlo, now what else do you have to tell me?" I told him that I had met with the US government in Washington recently and explained that we were in a new phase of reality, with agriculture supported by many farm-state Republicans. I also let him know that the media had been very supportive of the Cuban trade.

I told him the White House was in the middle of a review. I explained that Andy Card had put me in touch with Colonel Gonzalez, whom I met in Western Hemisphere Affairs. I informed him that the people deciding will be the president of the US, Karl Rove, and Condoleezza Rice, all under the chief of staff's guidance. There was no decision, and they were seriously considering an interim step granting farm equipment, which I believed was a positive sign.

I let him know that I had met with Andrew Natsios from USAID. I did not mention other government branches, except that my congressman and senators appeared to be positive on the issue but still required more work. I also expected that Jeb Bush might weigh in as well. The interest groups from South Florida and New Jersey would have their say, as well those from within the administration, Congress, and outside.

PHOTO 3.A. *From Left to Right, Pedro Alvarez, Fidel Casto, Juanita Vera, David with El Mappe, and Phil Olsson.*

He then turned to business. We had a two-hour discussion on feed and production practices of chickens, cows, and other farm animals. He understood protein and nutrition quite well. Fidel was looking to feed his populace. He said that he used a different type of grain instead of corn to lower the cost. Why can't we? He was supporting Pedro's efforts to buy cheap. I told him that I got the message loud and clear. He then turned the discussion to possibilities of extensions beyond farm equipment. Castro was unequivocal: "If you get rid of the embargo, we will give the United States of America the right of first refusal on everything sold to Cuba: agriculture, telecom, building supplies, equipment . . . everything." I knew this was several billion dollars to an economy worth marketing towards if done with proper credit constraints. I asked him about settling debts. He said, "I would absolutely settle every claim out there for peace between our nations."

I thought this was an excellent deal for the American people. I had the utmost respect for the Cuban exile community, and this deal would financially assist them, bury the hatchet, and move on profitably. I had to present this back to the White House.

I asked him about weapons of mass destruction and the possibility of inspections. Castro said, "Unequivocally, we have given airspace after 9/11, and we would have neutral third-party inspections of any site in Cuba. Cuba is a partner against the drug war, terrorism, and is for peace. Absolutely." I had some other questions but agreed to adjourn and discuss them another day.

When the meeting was over, we had lunch with Fidel. He spoke continuously for about four hours during and after our meal. He talked about political, cultural, and social issues. Phil Olsson and I left that day, looked at each other, and agreed not to discuss anything until we got away from security and went to the pool. We figured that if there were any place that may not be bugged or intruded on, it would be the pool.

With lit cigars, we looked at each other and said, "Oh my God." Phil looked at me and said, "Never in a million years would you expect that."

I had something to go back and discuss with the good colonel at the White House and the CIA.

Lesson Learned:

Overdeliver and keep swinging. Along the way, you will have the opportunity to make a sustainable difference in order to transform for a safer, new, and better world.

CHAPTER FOUR

Cuban-US Business Relations: From the Havana Expo to Beyond:
Humble Diplomatic Business and Blockbuster Accelerated Growth

Expo Hall

In late September of 2002, we purchased a booth at the Cuban Exposition for Food held in Havana. By that time, we had a slew of other companies that were part of the delegation we were representing. Publicly, Castro was welcoming the US agriculture delegation positively. He told Marc Frank, "I am very happy that they are coming. We have dealt with many of them, and they are people that really leave a good impression. They are excellent and educated people, and I have not seen any arrogance in any of them."[6] He spoke about discussions with ADM, Cargill, the US Chamber of Commerce, US Wheat Associates, USA Rice Federation, and my fellow boys and girls in the poultry associations.

Stephanie, my VP of HR, had not been with us a year yet when she took on the task of getting twenty-six OFAC-related federal licenses, housing, transportation, and round-trip flights to Cuba for the next trip. It was a monumental effort, and thankfully she did it flawlessly. After that, everything she did in the company was like eating birthday cake after chasing many small kids.

Some of the people who came on the trip were Jim Weatherly, Karl Frisch, and Carlos "BabaLou" Sanchez from Beaver Street Fisheries; Kathy and Don Pittman from Pittman Produce; Deb Yale, a broker from Maine; Rafi with Puerto Rican-Cuban-American Jorge Mayendia from Central Produce; attorneys Phil Olsson and Jerry Crawford; Stephanie; and several others.

By this time, the entire US food industry was there, including Tony DeLio and a delegation from ADM; "Marvin Lehrer's Rice Federation"; Jim Sumner, Greg Tyler, Jim Hoban, Jim Baker, Larry Lieberman, and Bob Breyan; Suj from Boston Agrex; David Hand from Pilgrim's Pride; Charlie Joyner from Dolphin Shipping; and a ton of boys from Tyson and Perdue. Orland Bethel was there from Hillandale Farms along with Howard Helmer, the World Record Omelet King, and a slew of congressmen and senators from the United States. It was a real dog and pony show the Cubans put on.

I was scheduled to meet with Fidel Castro several times during this visit. The first time was at the USAPEEC-American Egg Board meeting. At this meeting, Howard Helmer said, "Mr. President, I am so, so glad to meet you, and I wanted to present to you on behalf of the American Egg Board some bloopers that you may find funny!" Castro loved Howard, as everyone that ever has loves Howard. It was a two-hour meeting where Castro gave his rendition of the revolution and how he looked forward to working with the poultry and egg industry. He was welcoming of his new friends.

During this trip, we were in negotiations on our deal, which we planned to announce before the international press at the trade convention as the first US-Cuba food contract since the embargo. After the press conference, we also had plans to meet with the biotech folks, including Carlos Borroto and the PPG folks. The discussions with Pedro went very well, and we were looking to sign a deal the next morning for millions of eggs, including Born Free Organic, brown eggs fresh from New England, as well as white eggs. We got all three: Good, Better, and Best sold to Cuba, and we were going to get the press to broadcast our brands back to the United States.

Just as I finished with Alimport, a reporter from the NBC affiliate in Miami stopped by the booth and wanted an interview. I saw this as a potential minefield, but I took the interview because I have more guts than brains. She was solid in assessing the Cuban regime's oppression and wanted to know how I felt about supporting the regime where Cuban-American families had suffered from its brutality several decades earlier.

In this situation, I said that "I had the utmost respect for the Cuban exile community living in the Miami area, but I am here simply to sell United States eggs to pay my mortgage and some taxes." I was an American trying to earn a living. That is something I knew from working in the South Florida area previously with Cuban Americans like my attorneys Jose Casal, Juan Enjamio, and Raul Cosio from the law firm Holland & Knight in Miami. I also appreciate Rafael Kravec, a senior executive that was heavily involved with Shimon Peres and Jewish causes in Israel. Colonel Gonzalez made the connection for me. NBC used that soundbite. It's the best argument that we have that is understood by Cuban Americans.

Midnight Dinner

We met that night at the Presidential Palace at midnight. I was there with my delegation, and it was a fun, casual environment while King Fidel held court. It was a friendly diplomatic affair where we discussed family, politics, and life. I sat facing Fidel, and Jorge Meyandia sat to the far right on Castro's side with state security behind him. As President Reagan said, "Trust but verify."

We enjoyed lobster tails, salad, and great wine. The dinner lasted until 3:30 a.m. Fidel stood up and said it was time for bed. Then, he presented flowers to the women in the delegation. One unfortunate situation occurred. Jerry Crawford had money stolen, but we both agreed not to say anything because we feared the perpetrator's punishment. I told Jerry that I would take care of dinner at some point and make up for it. Jerry was a consummate politician but a liberal with a conscience in this matter. Later on, Jerry's firm helped with a personal situation involving a friend of my son, Ben, who was having challenges getting back into the country for school.

The Next Morning

Around 10:00 a.m., we were ready for the signing. We went to a table with the entire international press in attendance. I initially sat with Pedro for the signing. Orland Bethel and Howard Helmer were behind me to the right, and Castro was directly behind Pedro. John Kavulich, president of the US-Cuba Trade and Economic Council, was right in front of me facing the media. You see, newly arrived US Mission Chief Jim Cason made a statement of words to the effect of warning US businesses that the Cuban government's reputation was to not pay its bills, and they were a deadbeat in the world economy.

When I saw Fidel in the morning, he was a bit upset that the US mission chief was raining on his charm offensive parade. I signed the document as I watched Kavulich lip sync and point, "Have him sign." I listened to Kavulich, and as a reporter shouted out, "What do you think of Cason's comments?" I turned to Castro and said, "Mr. President, would you be kind enough to sign this document?" It was a monumental moment when Castro signed the agreement and held it high for the national press.

This event and the media were a big break for us. It raised our company's stature, brands, and industry. It was significant in executing our multi-tiered double- and triple-digit growth strategy found in the "Operational Excellence and Sustainability" sections in Chapters Four through Seven of *Principles of Cartel Disruption*, while expanding our international markets to Cuba. Fidel was now buying Born Free Organic Eggs from Pete and Jerry's of New Hampshire, brown eggs fresh from New England, and white eggs from America's Heartland—low-cost sustainable food shared with our new friends, the Cuban people. This deal was a win-win situation for the US industry and Cuba. We also turned Cason's threat into a tremendous opportunity to rise above it. If you genuinely want to be a sustainable leader, ensure that you bring along your industry friends. It can have so much more of an impact on repairing the world.

During my interview with NBC Miami, the reporter pressed hard and asked if it was true that I was concerned with payment and if that's why I had President Castro sign. I responded, "I am very comfortable with the US law and getting paid up front before we release any goods to the Cubans. We are not concerned at all. It brought a sense of goodwill that President Castro stood behind the purchases and payments."

Later, a British reporter from London asked me, "How do you feel being used by Castro and the Cubans for political purposes through these purchases?" After a full day with the media and a sleepless night, I shot back, "I would like to quote the poet Robert Seger from Michigan: "I used her. She used me. Neither one cared. We were getting our share." He looked at me after he wrote it down and said in a nice gentlemanly British voice, "Pardon me, Mr. Radlo, but I just can't write that." Then I came back with, "I am not going to say that it was necessarily appropriate for colonists to dump the British tea in the harbor that you were kind enough to bring to Boston to market several centuries ago, but we just simply don't have a problem marketing our farm products from the United States in the same fashion as Great Britain and the rest of the world have done for years with Cuba." I'm not sure if he used the entire quote. I'm glad he didn't print the Bob Seger quote, but it wasn't a bad comeback.

PHOTO 4.A. *Castro Lifting Signed Personal Guarantee in Front on our First Agreement Before the International Media:*

The Afternoon

Jerry Crawford, Phil Olsson, and I met with Castro in the afternoon. I invited Crawford because of his relationship with the Clintons. Jerry was a big deal in the Democratic Party. Because he was from Iowa, he had every Democratic candidate running for president staying at his house and sitting on his porch. His support was crucial to victories for the Clinton and Gore candidacies. More importantly, he had great personal relationships with people in the political world.

For this trip, Jerry had done his homework. He had polls showing how the Democratic Party's mood fared on the issue of ending travel restrictions and lifting the trade embargo. Castro liked that Jerry was connected to the Democratic Party and the Clintons.

I had a few questions that attorney Jose Casal of Holland & Knight wanted me to ask. They were as follows: Mr. President, do you believe in God, and what do you think about the pope? He was quite surprised and direct on the answer: "Daveed, look. My mother was an overbearing Catholic mother with strict rules on everything. If you don't do this, you are going to hell. If you don't do that, you are going to hell. Sooner or later, I realized that if I did not take out the trash, I was not going to hell. Personally, I am an agnostic, or perhaps a nonbeliever. Notwithstanding, I am a great believer that religion is good for the people, as it promotes morality. It absolutely will be supported by the Cuban people, and I certainly respect the pope."

Then, Jerry Crawford had a few questions to ask, and he kept copious notes. Jerry was concerned that our next meeting with Castro would interfere with making our plane on time. Castro said that it was not an issue. He would hold the plane until we were able to make it to the airport. Then, Phil Olsson shared a memory of a speech Castro gave at Harvard when he attended. Castro remembered it well and thanked Phil for providing that memory.

Castro answered every question with twenty-minute to one-hour answers. No one could say that he did not answer a question fully and comprehensively. At times, he would move to related subjects. Castro spoke with intelligence, humor, and passion. He was one of the most engaging people I've met in my life, plus he had tremendous charisma in running a nation. He also loves market research and does frequent polling of Cuban citizens on many different issues to keep current with the pulse.

His cartel regime could be ruthless and didn't tolerate dissidence. But if you were a Cuban that kept to yourself, worked hard, loved family, and did not rock the boat, you were in good straits. If you chose to cross the line in any fashion, you could end up in jail for a long time. If you hijacked a plane on Friday, you would be tried over the weekend and executed on Monday for the offense. I was with Castro a short time after a situation like that occurred, and Castro found it incredulous how we could spend so much money on lengthy trials and appeals when the remedy to such a horrible crime should be administered swiftly. Fidel was somewhere between a benevolent king and not your average Latin American dictator. In the words of Fidel, "History will absolve me." I'll let you decide.

PHOTO 4.B. *David with Fidel Castro and attorneys Jerry Crawford, on the left, and Phil Olsson, on the right.*

After meeting with Castro, we were shuttled back to our protocol house a few blocks from the town center near the Egyptian Embassy. It was a great location, and next to it was the exporter-importer of Habanos cigars worldwide. On a side note, the gentleman was quite an impressive guy with a remarkable brand and business.

Later that evening, I threw a cocktail party. I invited the entire US industry to Old Havana along with Alimport, the Cuban Foreign Ministry, the US Interests Section personnel, and perhaps some intelligence folks as well, with cocktails in their hands still listening. I could see the US State Department personnel felt a bit awkward, except for Susan Archer, who was usually friendly. I held the party at Restaurante Santo Ángel. There was a great showing, and the entire US industry appreciated the outreach by our company.

Jim Sumner came up to me and said, "Daveed, you outdid yourself. You pulled a rabbit out of the hat this morning before the press." I said to Jim, "*Muchas gracias, todo bien.*" Jim, the ever-consummate politician, noticed, as I did too, the tension in the air between the Cuban Foreign Ministry and the US Interests Section personnel. I said to Jim, "I think we need to get everyone a few more drinks, and they will either learn to get along or perhaps throw a few punches to get it out of them." "Daveed," Jim said with a smile, "not sure it would be diplomatic protocol, but it sure would be fun to see."

Greg Tyler was the first to show appreciation whenever an event was sponsored for the industry. He always was dignified and respectful in that way. After the cocktail party was over, I caught up with the men and women from USAPEEC but went back early because it had been a hell of a long day. The next morning, after a great Café Cubano of latte and coffee along with a shot of espresso, we headed to biotech land. We learned more about their technology and what drugs they were willing to present to OFAC for approval to import. At the same time, we went to see the PPG folks.

We had an exciting night planned, and our instructions were to return early. A vehicle took us to a special function room near the Palco and near where we stayed. When I got my seat assignment this time, I was sitting next to First Vice President Carlos Lage. Castro was sitting with Governor Jesse Ventura, Jim Sumner, and other heads of the industry. I spent several hours with Lage discussing the correct way to handle poverty in the world. I spent quite a bit of time researching the subject and received counsel on African affairs from Andrew Natsios when I met with him at USAID. The Cubans were serious about working internationally to aid in sustainable development in Africa, and the Cubans praised the Carter Center for their work there. He also shared the partnership they had throughout Latin America and South America, especially with Venezuela, to train doctors and researchers in medicine. He discussed their commitment to the biotech industry, and overall it was a thought-provoking discussion on the Cuban heart and soul professionally on policy. I was impressed with Lage.

Meanwhile, the entire US industry had a night that couldn't be put back in a bottle. It was an evening of the best entertainment I have ever witnessed in my life. First, the choreographed serving of dinner was both elegant and efficient, with a high volume of well-dressed, attractive Cuban women quickly serving courses of meals. Second, the performers were out of this world. Pianist Chucho Valdés and Buena Vista Social Club performed and brought the house down. Also, an array of Latin American jazz and blues followed. There was a ballet performance of extraordinary talent. The food was exquisite, and the entertainment was beyond world-class.

The Cubans outdid themselves, and everyone in the US agriculture industry left with additional support for business and growing our relationship with this nation. It was not the socialistic, nationalistic speeches; it was not pounding the tables; it was that charming night that mattered. Tony DeLio remarked to me, "David, you can't take this back. US-Cuba relations will never be the same. We are progressing, and nothing will stop us."

The next morning, Luis, who took orders from the entire US delegation, came back to fulfill his order requests, and everyone received two boxes of cigars worth about $50, with a receipt because we needed the receipt to get back in the US. Anyone who tried to sneak back more ran the risk the cigars would get confiscated, and your record could be marked.

Then, I headed off to see Susan Archer and Jim Cason at the US Interests Section. Jim paid homage to me for the follow-up to his remarks. We had a fascinating discussion, where Jim shared his background, education, what he learned about Cuba, and shared the party line on US policy. As noted earlier, I called it, "What would my parents and grandparents think about Cuban-American diplomacy?" Most Cuban Americans say that to you when you bring up the validity of ending travel restrictions and the embargo, despite the insistence that there was a shred of real US diplomacy with the Cuban policy, which Cason so eloquently stated. I was quick to smile and say, "Cut the bullsh-t, Jim. You need to be savvy enough to read the tea leaves. This is about a special interest that has been loyal to a specific candidate and party in a critical swing state. That is what we were dealing with.

Most people that came from the States spent their time refuting the policy bullsh-t that the State Department and others in the government put out. I am using the word bullsh-t because that is what a prominent US congressman characterized it as. Our policy, which perhaps we wished changed, was US law, and there were lots of Cuban Americans that lost family members and friends several years ago who were shot. I guess the lucky ones left Cuba penniless with homes. Their property couldn't be sold and became confiscated by the state. But for God's sake, ladies and gentlemen, boys and girls, be straight about it. It's a divorce battle between the same family in Cuba and Florida, with some living in New Jersey, and US industry is caught in the crosshairs of the divorce."

Cason smiled. Then he asked whether we would be interested in helping with the Frosty the Snowman holiday display and Christmas decorations. I said that I would be happy to help. I just needed to know how much and when. Our company bought specific Christmas decorations along with Frosty and had them shipped to the State Department. I had no idea later that Frosty and a Christmas tree would be in the middle of an international dispute, but we will leave that for a bit later. I learned that Jim could be one hell of a creative troublemaker.

I was impressed with Cason's knowledge of Latin America. He had a reputation for standing up to dictators left or right. He had no trouble poking his finger in the dictators' eyes as he did the previous day, to which I had to respond. The reality was that the State Department disagreed with the TSRA, but they liked us and on their next assignment broke the doors down to help us.

In this situation, they had a slightly different mission. But we all were Americans, and Cuba was still officially the enemy. As my great friend Kevin Cloherty, deputy general counsel at John Hancock-Manulife, and former head of the New England Organized Crime Strike Force, pointed out to me, "Medical marijuana is legal in many states so that doctors may prescribe the active ingredient, THC, but it is still an illegal federal drug, and you could go to jail for it." The federal law is the law, and we have to respect it as much as we may respectfully disagree.

Some Americans had different opinions, but many Cubans became our friends. It was incumbent on us to love our enemies. Thank you, Dr. King. We can get more done through constructive engagement and talking than we can by hitting for hitting and hating for hating and cutting off relations. It's only a cheaper and better alternative. As usual, I found myself reflecting on Professor Jim Elliot from Tufts, who was my advisor and political philosophy professor, and Aristotle's "Golden mean between extremes." Notwithstanding, in the middle, you can get an awful lot done.

Some diplomats deserve specific mention. The first is the Cuban Interests Section chief to the United States (the unofficial Cuban ambassador to the United States), Dagoberto Rodriguez. He was a nice, straight guy, who Olsson later had over for dinner at his house. Another is Charles Stenholm, who just left the House after many years. Charlie was an ardent supporter of agriculture and a conservative Democrat who lost the 2004 midterm election, which changed the tenor between Democrats and Republicans. Agriculture lost a great friend in Congress.

Gustavo Machín also deserves mention. Gustavo's dad, who died fighting in the revolution with Fidel, was a consummate politician and a prince of darkness. Gustavo is a Paul Shapiro type that you will learn about later in this book, exceedingly bright and savvy. The US eventually threw Gustavo out of the United States for spying. I was invited once to Dagoberto's residence for dinner before Olsson reciprocated. I had a feeling that the CIA had the house bugged. I got a call about a week later to meet with the CIA. They wanted to know what business I had with Dagoberto. I asked them directly whether they would help us import medical, pharmaceutical intellectual property from Cuba through the State Department and the Treasury Department's Office of Foreign Asset Control (OFAC) process. They laughed at me and said, "So it's a business deal. Sorry, we can't help you." The CIA was a one-way street. I found the CIA to be exceedingly straight. They were going to report to Congress and the administration precisely what they were hearing or found. It was not going to be a Cuban-American whitewash snow job for political purposes. The stakes were too high following 9/11, the Gulf War, the War in Afghanistan, and the soon-to-be incursion into Iraq. They were going to be fair and unbiased based upon the available intelligence. Frankly, it was refreshing.

I knew where the line was with these guys. The Cubans were diplomats of the Cuban government that were under continuous surveillance by the US intelligence services. Of course, our diplomats in Havana were under similar surveillance. It was part of this diplomatic chess match and gamesmanship. When Gustavo and two others were removed from the country for spying, I was happy to understand where the line was.

Now, as stakeholders in the US, we have spent trillions of dollars and left tens of billions of dollars of sophisticated arms in addition to life, limb, and brain-related trauma in Afghanistan. We've turned over the country to a group with a reputation for supporting terrorism and having relationships and sympathy with other terrorist groups. They also have a history of treating women less progressively. Further, we have closed the door to economic relationships that may have helped pay back what we spent there and handed it over to China and others. According to military sources, we no longer have adequate means of intelligence in the country. We pulled out our base presence and a few thousand troops as we watched the Afghanistan government topple.

Currently, the country has issues with refugees, and the Taliban is pursuing people who helped the US. A Democrat and former Marine officer in Iraq, Seth Moulton, made a 2021 bi-partisan trip during the exit from Afghanistan. I supported his election to Congress. Seth characterized the withdrawal from Afghanistan as a "Total f-cking disaster!" in New York Magazine on August 26, 2021. This situation is not exactly leading to a safer, new, and better world. History will repeat itself if you ignore the lessons of the past.

Now, Back to Cuba.

It was about this time that I received a call from Mary-Jo Adams. She was working with Frank Phillips and his wife on one of the fully endorsed Cuban-US projects. It was the cultural project of the restoration of Ernest Hemingway's home in Cuba. They were looking for seed capital and advice to get things rolling. They felt with seed capital that they could steamroll as people saw the effects of the restoration of Ernest Hemingway's boat *Pilar*, from which he spotted German U-boats off the coast of Cuba during World War II, in addition to his fine home. I told them I would reinvest profits from Cuban sales into this venture.

Several years later, when we were against the wall with a potentially deadly global story on salmonella, I reached out to Frank to give me a character reference, and I greatly appreciated it. I was not looking for that when I jumped in to help the Hemingway Preservation Foundation, which became the Finca Vigía Foundation (https://fincafoundation.org), but it was quite fortunate.

I was later able to see the fantastic restoration, and guess what? My uncle Andre Kostelanetz's record was playing on Ernest Hemingway's record player by chance. I saw the seat where Hemingway used to write longhand by a window looking out on a field where he played baseball with youths from the neighborhood. On a much later trip to Cuba, I went back with my temple's congregation in 2015. We brought gloves, bats, and balls to distribute to youths in cooperation with a man whom Ernest Hemingway once played ball with.

Cuba was such an interesting place, with outstanding arts, culture, an educated populace, medical and biotech areas, and engaging personalities. It was also exceedingly poor in certain regions. They did not stop older people from leaving the island because Cuba does not have a Socialist program to care for the low-income elderly.

The other charity that I quietly took part in was both the joint distribution committee for the Jewish people in Cuba, bringing them vitamins and certain other supplies needed, and Catholic Charities. There was a real opportunity to help people in Cuba, and it was the right thing to do it.

www.jdc.org

www.friendsofcaritascubana.org

After the Exposition

We had some excellent follow-up press from this Cuba trip internationally. It also provided a superb promotional vehicle for our business to grow sales, markets, and new products in Cuba. We left with not only an ample supply of Cuban cigars but also some extraordinary stories to discuss the personal side of Fidel Castro. It made for some interesting beer conversations at conventions.

I shared the ride back from Cuba on a subsequent trip with US diplomat

Susan Archer. Susan had finished her tour and was going back to Washington. I appreciated the tireless work she and other diplomats did to serve as a beachhead for folks from the US in a foreign land and with the ferrying through of Visa requests to come to the United States, not to mention their aiding the intelligence efforts on economic and political conditions. It isn't easy to go from country to country.

She left her boyfriend in Cuba and would start out fresh somewhere else, either on an assignment in Washington or other lands. I gave Susan a big hug in Miami, and that was the last I saw of her.

I had further discussions in Washington with Colonel Gonzalez. As the administration was more settled in their policy and presented the need to Congress, he said he would need specific conditions to bring back to the White House personnel. Overall, the emphasis was turning towards the Iraq situation.

On a subsequent trip to Cuba, Jim Cason introduced me to Susan Archer's replacement. She looked like someone I had seen before but couldn't place where I would have met her. Her name was Usha Pitts, and she was a very attractive woman. She appeared to be tough as nails. She had just come from an assignment in the US Embassy in Russia. After quite a bit of talking, I found out that she grew up a few miles away from me in Concord and Acton, Massachusetts. Her dad was a professor at the University of Massachusetts Amherst. It was likely that I had seen her before and may have spoken to her as well. She was in Cuba with her two children and husband, whom she met in Italy on an assignment. I got to know Usha quite well over the next few years as she helped Jim Cason stir up a ruckus on the island.

Soon after that, I brought the Maine delegation to Cuba. I met with Fidel for several hours, but this time with Bill Bell, Senator John Nutting, Don Hoenig, Deb Yale, and a few other Mainers. Fidel was exceedingly gracious. He signed autographs and everyone left with the diplomatic cigar package. Later on the trip, Jim Cason hosted us at the US Interests Section residence for dinner. The residence was expanded with an elevator to benefit FDR as he was planning to visit when WWII started. Although he did not come, I had the distinct honor to sit in the seat that Winston Churchill sat in when he visited Cuba and the US Mission. It was one of the most elegant home-cooked meals I had ever had.

In the back of the residence was a vegetable garden where Jim had worked during the weekend. He also introduced legal US-Cuban tobacco. He was an exceptional organic farmer. He was in the middle of a book that he was finishing in tribute to the history of the US Mission residence in Cuba. I told him that when he was finished, I would be honored if I could purchase a copy.

I got to know Usha quite well and shared a trip from Miami over to Havana with her once. It was then that I learned from her what it was like to be a diplomat in Havana. She said that Cuban security would regularly go through her clothes at home and move things from one side of the closet to the other. It was the normal hassle they did. She said that she enjoyed Cuba, which had a great international diplomatic community. Her family was more liberal than the entire Massachusetts congressional delegation that called for the embargo's end and the lifting of travel restrictions. Castro referred to the delegation's policies as due to being geographically located closest to Europe. Usha was on the US team, and she was a lifelong career

PHOTO 4.C. *Jim Cason, US ambassador (Interests Section chief) with Howard Helmer of the American Egg Board at the Food Expo in 2002. The PS from Cason's note reads, "Don't leave your eggs in one basket."*

diplomat; It seemed she enjoyed the fight quite a bit, and she enjoyed the challenge of working with Jim Cason.

On a subsequent trip, I met with Usha at the Hotel Nacional. Cuban security found out, and I was confronted with it. Usha did not have friends in Cuba. The people she interacted with were either teammates with the State Department or Cuban nationals. So, when I came to visit, I did what I do best: I acted as the executive growth coach and Trusted Advisor in addition to being a sustainable diplomatic leader.

Later, I was confronted by Ministry officials with Pedro. I told them about how Usha and I grew up together in Massachusetts. The Cubans were concerned about meeting with lower-level diplomats that were held to different standards in the diplomatic war and chess match between the Cuban government's Foreign Ministry and the State Department. Once they understood that we had preexisting roots, with her family living close to mine in Massachusetts, they backed off their concerns. You see, diplomats are usually under constant surveillance by Cuban security forces. They felt embarrassed that they did not research our backgrounds, and we received an apology. I never got flack from the Cubans for meeting with Jim Cason. He was the highest-ranking US official on the island, and despite their aversion to what the US and at times Cason did, they never held it against me.

On one occasion, a US live animal exporter confronted me on the sixth floor of the Hotel Nacional. He had heard that I met with Cason and supported the

Christmas display at the US mission. He was furious about it. He said words to the effect of, "You're a son of a bitch for doing so. Do you know who I am? Do you know about my family and how we [our cartel] controlled America?"

I looked him in the eyes and said, "I will meet with representatives of the United States government anytime that I choose, and I won't comment further that you, as part of the original cartel, were against a US citizen meeting with the highest-ranking US official in a foreign country. Further, I don't give a damn about how f-cking wealthy your family is because the money is made on the backs of people like my immigrant grandfather that slaved away in your factories. You should be thanking me and not cursing me for exercising my freedom and liberties where our great nation was founded."

I then informed Pedro and Alex, who equally were upset by the interaction. I let them deal with the cartel guy. I was one of the few US agriculture people doing business with Cuba that also supported the US government despite their congressional- and White House-mandated policy. You can't be narrow-minded, folks. Don't let the trees get in the way of seeing the forest. You will need these diplomats wherever you are. They were helpful when a member of the delegation became ill, and they did outstanding service throughout the world as civil servants.

Provocation at Cason's Residence

After the trade fair, the business was going well. The press was in our favor. When I saw a member of the Bush administration responsible for Cuba, he said they would do their best to accommodate us and continue working in good faith on the farm equipment. However, he let me in the door and said, "We give you guys everything around the world and support you big; we also have lowered your taxes and reduced regulation. We need Cuba." I heard a voice that sounded a lot like the political guru at the White House.

As it turned out, the president kicked the issue to his brother Jeb, the governor of Florida, and they were starting to move in that direction quietly. I countered and said, "Please look at the opportunity for billions of dollars in trade. This is not millions; this is billions that will greatly help US business and the economy. What would it take to bring about peace?"

Colonel Gonzalez brought up a few old issues, including the possible extradition of JoAnne Chesimard, who killed a New Jersey state trooper. Then he said the phrase, "What would my father think?" *Here we go again*, I thought. We finally get to the real issue that separates the US from having excellent relations with Cuba. "What would my (Cuban-American) father, mother, and grandparents think?"

I held this at bay when I went back to Cuba. I met with Castro right after

Cason let seventy-five dissidents onto his property in the first quarter of 2003. Republican presidents from Nixon, Ford, Reagan, H. W. Bush, and W. Bush took a hostile approach towards Cuba, and now Cason had deliberately provoked a response by inviting dissidents to his residence. Castro told me he had "no choice but to react to this deliberate provocation." He went into great detail about the history of the US and Cuba.

The press was brutal on the crackdown, and the Cuban Americans were striking back at the charm offensive. John Kavulich described the situation as "checkbook diplomacy." It was a strategic move of neoconservatives and Cuban-American activists in the State Department of Otto Reich and Dan Fisk, along with support from the White House. They were asserting the Cuban-American and neoconservative position on Cuba, which conflicted with the economic position that us doing trade with Cuba espoused.

I went to see Cason and said, "Jim, what the hell are you doing? You knew that all these people would be thrown in jail for a long time for doing this. He then said with a smile, "David, I am sure Jesse Jackson or someone else will come over and liberate them." I could see the wheels turning. It was the counteroffensive on behalf of the Cuban-American community that desired to keep the embargo and travel restrictions and make it harder to do business in Cuba. It was also the seeds that benefited the unofficial committee to reelect the president, Havana Bureau. The Cuban Americans later followed up industry lobbying with new political interest contributions on their side. They launched their counteroffensive just as US industry was starting to threaten the political status quo of the Cuban-American community. They needed the leverage back against Castro and with the media. They also got unanimous reasoning among the state administration, including USAID, as Andrew's deputy was Cuban Adolpho Franco. They lined up with a unified approach of isolation and increased restrictions in line with the president's May speech that outlined steps to ratchet up pressure on the Cuban government.

The White House took into consideration that we could have attained billions of dollars in business from Cuba and the opportunity to ensure third-party inspections of biotech facilities as echoed by State Department neoconservative John Bolton, but the reality was that our economic position in industry was being outweighed by the Cuban-American interest groups, along with Florida and New Jersey politics. It appeared the administration was locked in after the dissident issue and the president's speech.

White House sources unofficially told me if the CIA couldn't provide us with the correct information about Cuba, then we needed to check with the DIA (Defense Intelligence Agency) or some other intelligence bureau. As we learned, when any administration chooses a policy agenda, it becomes an issue of marketing and gaining support for their position based on the best analysis. The same agenda support was carried out for the Iraq War by the Bush administration. Many on both sides of the aisle supported it based on the available intelligence. Behind the iron curtain, the list of our enemies needed improvement.

The Iraq War

The business was going well in Cuba and continued for a few years with the United States. In 2003, I was able to meet with Castro shortly before the war commenced. The cat was out of the bag on US policy towards Cuba. When I initially got to Cuba, Pedro met with me quickly and said, "What are you hearing?" I was very direct. "All the BS that you hear in the media and from the State Department comes down to one thing on US policy. The situation is an interest group domestic policy issue, not an international one.

"Whatever is good for the Cuban-American interest groups that backed President and Governor Bush is good for America. The administration felt that industry could survive without Cuba, so the food, agriculture, and medicine folks that sell to Cuba would understand their allegiance to Cuban Americans and still support them given the administration's support domestically and worldwide. That's it, Pedro. 'What would my parents and grandparents think? Foreign diplomacy.'"

He then said, "Oh, that's not what we are hearing from other people."

A secretary came into the room and motioned with his hands over the lower part of his face signaling the bearded leader was on the phone. When Pedro returned, he told me the president looked forward to seeing me and discussing more. When I met with Castro, I was direct. Perhaps I was too blunt for a man that desperately wanted to leave his legacy in the world as making peace with the United States and bury the hatchet with the Cuban Americans by settling claims and moving forward with more commerce and reduction of travel restrictions.

I had a political theory discussion with Castro. I discussed how we based our system on how "politics flow from economics," as Harrington had said. He countered with, "*Politicos de economicos, o economicos de politicos.* In Cuba, Daveed, I will let you decide which comes first."

Photo 4.D. Lunch with Pedro Alvarez, Fidel Castro, and Phil Olsson

"*Yo comprendo, Senor Presidente*," I said.

We sat down, and there were two armed security guards near me. Frankly, I didn't know what he was going to do to me. I was direct with him and stated that we were dealing with an internal interest group advocation issue in the states. Florida especially was a key interest group that controlled the Florida governorship and White House.

It was an internal US political matter. The Cubans in the United States had a power that manifested itself in political support and payback for such support. I knew that it would not be pleasant telling the president of Cuba that the United States wanted to continue the cold war and may look to ratchet things up even more. I raised the White House issues, emphasizing freeing dissidents and releasing JoAnne Chesimard. This escapee was involved with murdering a New Jersey state trooper, and it was clear that they were not going to move towards peace until there was a resolution of old issues.

Castro said to me, "Radlo, I have listened to you. Now you listen to me." He went on for an hour, first dealing with the Chesimard issue. He said she was a wonderful grandmother, and she was staying put. The other issues were not constructive to dialogue, as the United States had started the provocation with the dissidents. He discussed the US for its historical policy, especially towards Republican presidents. Castro said that Carter, who had recently come to Cuba, was a partner in progress and believed Clinton was also supporting the TSRA. However, he said something to the effect that H. W. and W. Bush were "like Batista. When they die, they will end up with the devil, and he will have a difficult decision of which circle of hell would be appropriate for their purpose." *Uh oh*, I thought. He stated that they were disgraceful and merely puppets for a select few in Miami.

He then discussed the former dictator, Fulgencio Batista, propped up by the United States, and how he had brought forth the revolution to depose him on his soil. He again referred to political theory on Dante and the circles of hell in his famous speech "History Will Absolve Me." He said Reagan, H. W. Bush and W. Bush belong in that circle of hell as well, along with the CIA, who tried to kill him for many years, as well as Nixon, who wanted to really invade if he beat Kennedy and not just the Bay of Pigs sideshow. He said that he had not cashed one check from the United States on Guantanamo Bay's unlawful possession, nor will he ever. I thought that Phil Olsson and I would be escorted to the plane or jail. Pedro and I left the meeting, and he just shook his head and said with a smile, "Oh, boy."

Support of Troops in Iraq

I was in Cuba during the Iraq War and was in consistent contact with my good friend, Colonel Robert McLaughlin, who did multiple war-theatre tours and was in Iraq at the time. I received updates on the casualty report, ceremonies for the heroes lost in battle, and we had an in-depth discussion about keeping up morale for those who had their terms extended in the fighting, as the troops also wrestled at times with post-traumatic stress disorder (PTSD). We did whatever we could to support their effort with Stephanie's assistance, including regularly sending care packages, phone cards, mixed dried fruit, candy, and personal care products. He said that when they arrived, it was like a holiday for the troops. We worked hard to keep these holidays coming. It was the least we could do to show support for the soldiers. I went into detail about the importance of giving back with your time, talents, contacts, and finance in Chapter Eleven of *Principles of Cartel Disruption.* Supporting our troops in battle is at the top of the list. In a later promotion, he held the assignment of chief of staff for US forces in Afghanistan. The colonel sent warm greetings from Afghanistan's front line when he found out about my former WWII GI father's passing. He recognized my father's service as heroic. He was tied up with more important things, but Colonel Bob McLaughlin reached out and sent us a note immediately, and it meant so much to our family.

Castro's Charm Offensive Strategy

Castro believed with the start of committing aid after a hurricane that "politics stops at the water's edge, and goodwill would beget goodwill." H. W. Bush eloquently made this statement in his 1989 inaugural address. Castro committed to buying food and medicine under the TSRA right after the US offered aid for hurricane relief in 2001. He realized that there were forces for change, but the change would not occur as fast, and he was deeply hurt by the hardline presidential administration of George W. Bush.

Blute and Hamilton after Baghdad Fell

Castro was upset after Baghdad fell. He had a close relationship with Sadam Hussein. When the Iraqi dictator was ill, Castro sent him a team of doctors and a few boxes of cigars. I brought the media with me and was about to meet with Fidel. Then, two of the media members "crossed the line" and met with a dissident. Jim Cason arranged the meeting. The media members were upset when informed they wouldn't get to meet with Fidel. I told them that they had made a conscious choice to meet with the dissidents. They could not have both.

We continued to get great press from Mary Murray's NBC News, which featured stories about doing business with Cuba. There was also great press from Robin Hamilton of *Boston* magazine and NBC affiliate WBZ in Boston, which former Congressman Peter Blute of the WEEI radio station generated.

Great Intern Experience

As noted as well in Chapter Eleven of *Principles of Cartel Disruption*, I am a big believer in giving back through internships for college students. I had one intern named Matt Keller, an athlete from Tufts University and the DU fraternity. First, Matt had the opportunity to attend one of the greatest football games ever; it was called the Snow Bowl during the 2001–02 season. The Patriots beat the Oakland Raiders with an Adam Vinatieri kick during a snowstorm to advance in the playoffs and eventually made it to the Super Bowl. Matt ended up getting a job through his contacts at this meeting.

In 2003, Matt had the opportunity to go to Cuba with me and our delegation. He attended a state dinner with Fidel and the Foreign Ministry held at the Presidential Palace. Matt met many people on that trip and said it was one of the most memorable experiences of his life. He experienced a tremendously interesting and educational experience in nationalism. Giving back is essential, as noted in the 11th Principle of cartel disruption in my first book.

2004 December: Christmas Display Fight

On another occasion, we had a meeting with Pedro and Alex to sew up a strong deal. I went to the Foreign Ministry's Alimport office, which had been an old Buick dealership before the revolution in Havana. Unknowingly, Jim Cason was up to his old tricks. Previously, with our assistance, he added a Frosty the Snowman and Christmas tree to his holiday display. For the past two years, the Cubans had tolerated his decorations, and frankly, at night, it was a shiny glow on Havana's Malecón, which was the road along the water where many lovers spent time.

Then, Cason added a large circle with the number 75 inside of it, referring to the number of Cuban dissidents taken into state custody. In addition, he added a replica of a small cell to represent the dissident prisoners held in jail. This was too much for the Cubans; they went crazy. They summoned Jim to the Foreign Ministry, demanded that he take down the Christmas display, and threatened that he would be expelled the next day if he did not. I didn't know what was happening. Pedro and Alex, the ever-present businessmen that like me did not want politics to get in the way of good business, asked me, "Will you ever come back?" I said, "Of course I will."

I called Jim, and he invited me over to dinner at the residence. I ended up slipping out of the Hotel Nacional where I was staying and caught a random taxi—just an old beat-up 1950s Ford—and went to the residence. The conversation over dinner went something like this: "Jim, what the f-ck did you do now?" He explained in great detail, and he was, for the first time, quite sad and reflective over his time in Havana.

In the late part of his tenure, he called himself Cabo Cason and drove to diplomat parties with a Cabo Cason flag on his car instead of one from the US. He also grew Cabo Cason US free tobacco since the US residence is officially on US soil. I think he did this for the disdain of people like me that were not allowed to bring back new cigars as part of the increased regulations against the Cuban government. Tragically, the regulations only allowed a family to visit every three years. Many people weren't able to see sick or dying family or friends because of the travel ban, and it also stopped hard currency from coming into the country.

Cason knew the Cubans would react negatively. So, before they did, he got word to the State Department's senior level and told them what had happened. In Washington, the State Department backed Cason in a big way and issued a statement about how Castro and the Cubans had declared war on Frosty the Snowman, a Christmas tree, and Christmas. I thought I was part of an international incident and the diplomatic conflict between the US and Cuba. All I did was provide them with Frosty and Christmas decorations. I couldn't believe what it had turned into, which was a cover to show how upsetting the conditions were for dissidents. Instead of throwing Cason out, the Cubans placed a billboard next to the US Embassy with images of Iraqis in the Abu Ghraib prison allegedly being abused by US soldiers, with the word "fascists" written on it. It also had swastikas displayed on it.

Soon after that, Castro headed a million-man worker march along the Malecón that ended right in front of the US Interests Section. He delivered speeches against the evil imperialist forces of the United States, George W. Bush, and his administration. Miraculously, Cabo Cason survived. Castro even admitted to me once that he could get upset beyond what he desired, and then he would cool down.

I met with Jim one more time before he left, and from then on, he was the absolute hero of the Cuban-American community. I told him that he was in the Havana office of the Republican National Committee and the Committee to Re-elect the President. Cason smiled but reminded me that he was simply a believer in the anti-dictator party and would take on the left or right. He didn't care. He also lived in South Florida, and I thought he had an eye on a congressional run and political office. I was not totally wrong in that regard. When Cabo Cason left Cuba in 2005, he could've taken any assignment. The Cuban Americans, State Department, the Republican National Committee, and the Committee to Re-elect the President loved him.

From 2004–05, I was able to make pleas to the higher-ups in the Foreign Ministry and Castro to release a few Americans held as prisoners. The Foreign Ministry told me that they had irrefutable evidence that the American citizens had engaged in fueling dissident and insurrection activities. I told them that it was one thing to jail your own citizens, but they were your citizens. In this instance, these people were in fact US citizens, and the president of Cuba said himself that US citizens were guests in his country. The way to deal with guests that you don't like is to allow them to leave the party and not invite them to a new one.

There were many pleadings and follow-up conversations with the Cuban Foreign Ministry and the Cuban government's senior levels. The State Department appreciated the fruitful assistance and sent a letter to me in this regard. Despite his criticism of the Castro regime, Andrew Natsios smiled and said, "That's good work."

EMBASSY OF SWITZERLAND
UNITED STATES OF AMERICA INTERESTS SECTION
Calzada Between L & M Streets, Vedado
Havana, Cuba
September 1, 2005

Mr. David Radlo
President and CEO
RADLO FOODS, LLC.
313 Pleasant Street
Watertown, MA 02472

Dear David,

Thank you very much for the support you have given to further the case of Human Rights in Cuba.

It is with extreme gratitude that I express not only for the financial support for the Interest Section's Holiday Display, but the direct appeals to the highest levels in the Cuban Government on behalf of dissidents and U.S. citizens imprisoned (some which were met with success).

I fully realize the price you and your company may have paid through both reduction of access to the higher levels of the GOC and perhaps loss of direct business.

Shalom.

Sincerely,

James C. Cason
Chief of Mission

EXHBIT 4.E.

After Jim Cason left Cuba, he settled to be ambassador to Paraguay because he needed rest from his intense assignment in Cuba. His book on the US residence was great, and he began learning an old obscure language in Paraguay as he immersed himself in the new culture. Cason later took a higher position with the State Department consulting on diplomatic affairs. Then he ran for mayor of Coral Gables, Florida. I supported and met him for dinner in Coral Gables not long ago. Yes, we sold specialty eggs to South Florida for a long time, and we appreciated the business. Jim had the rare combination of being both extraordinarily bright and creative. I always appreciated him for that combination.

In 2005 and 2006, there was increased support from Cuban-American interest groups to tighten restrictions with Cuba. The administration changed their policy of payments at OFAC. It shifted to cash up front from cash against documents (CAD); CAD meant you could ship to Cuba, but you had to receive payment before the goods could be released. With the "OFAC clarification" of CAD elimination and the insistence of payment up front before the ship left or a letter of credit was issued, the Cuban government felt it necessary to react. The Cubans responded by eliminating what they called "cash and carry." This policy meant that if they continued to import large commodities like chicken leg quarters, grains, and feed, they would stop importing all other items.

Thanks to the regulations that came forth from the US government, several million dollars in business with Cuba ended for our industry. We hoped a new administration would change the future policy, but for now, it was time to focus on other markets, while my poultry and feed friends accelerated business. The Bush administration also curtailed cultural exchange trips along with visits by Cuban Americans to see their families. What did Fleetwood Mac say? "Oh well, oh well, oh well."

Where Are They Now?

I went back to Cuba on a cultural exchange trip with my temple a short time ago as a new US administration allowed it. I visited Hemingway's residence, where I am still a board advisor, and it was close to being finished. His boat, which found the German U-boat during WWII, was impeccable. The living room still had Uncle Andre Kostelanetz's record playing. Also, we were able to provide bats and gloves to the kids living near the house. The excitement in their eyes from receiving bats, balls, and gloves was undoubtedly something that I will remember for life.

We also had the opportunity to view the most compelling Cuban art that I had ever seen, both in drawings as well as an area that artists created. We stayed at the Hotel Nacional. Mary Murray was still in Cuba, but NBC changed their offices to another location from the sixth floor of the Hotel Nacional. I was able to see Luis, who was kind enough to sell the delegation certain cigars. We also had the opportunity to meet with the Jewish community leader. The Jewish population was once quite large but has diminished to a few hundred. Ironically, the banned religious practice is now encouraged. Cuban citizens are now allowed to go to Israel. Many Jews visit and don't return. The legend is that Cubans are excommunicated Sephardic Jews and have a tremendous work ethic that stems from the old country.

One day, I will go back to go fishing when it is legal. I understand that Cuba has outstanding fishing. However, the fishing off of Florida is fantastic as well. I think that is part of the embargo rationale from Florida. They don't want Cuba's competition when snowbirds like me like to go to Florida for vacation. I have traveled in Cuba in a relatively small section from Varadero to Havana, but the focus was on business and enjoying the culture.

To go from one side of Cuba to the other could take thirteen to sixteen hours. That's more than going from Boston to Washington, DC. I once got into the water for a swim, but the Cuban authorities forced me out of the water because they thought I would leave the island and try to swim across to Florida or the Keys. Water seems to be a place that you can get into trouble in Cuba, so I did what I could to avoid it.

Meanwhile, Pedro allegedly built a nice retirement reserve while at Alimport. Sources close to Cuban government officials said that his daughter arrived on a boat one day after his wife had shockingly died. She stayed for a visit for several days. When it came time for her to leave, Pedro took her to dinner. Then, he brought several suitcases to the boat. Pedro did something that Meyer Lansky forgot to do. He may have taken some of the retirement money in the luggage out of the country. According to sources, an informant in Cuba related to Cuban security said they found some of the money still left in Pedro's home. It happened just before he was to take a protocol position and assist with guest housing assignments. The rumor was that he was either somewhere in the Tampa area or Spain. It was nice of Pedro to give the fatherland an exit tax deposit just before he left for good . . . allegedly.

As US agriculture's philosophical business "Bad Boy" Jack DeCoster said, "A man isn't worth much unless he cheats and steals a little. The problem with mankind is that when someone steals a little, they end up stealing a lot. You get caught. Yes, sirree, you do." I am delighted that Pedro is spending time with his family that he left and that he was able to get away with a bit more than Meyer Lanksy. I am on the side that all income received was well earned and deserved but other sources that I have spoken to characterize it differently. Whether that is Communist propaganda or truth, I really do not know. I'll let you decide.

PHOTO 4.F. *Vivian Alvarez, David, and Pedro Alvarez (president of Alimport)*

As for Alex, I still keep in touch from time to time. He could have jumped the pond and been an exceptionally financially wealthy person if he went to Miami, given his ability to negotiate. He could have gotten a law degree or stayed in business. However, Alex put his family first and continues to live in Havana, at times in Mexico in business, but has left Alimport.

Luis is still going to shul every day, continues to sell cigars, and continues to stay in touch, having never missed a holiday to wish my family well. He has also been able to come to the United States and see his family in Miami and North Carolina. He is a citizen of Poland now as Cuba allows dual citizenship.

As for Fidel, he was at best like Moses and never made it to the promised land. He outlived several US presidents and the many US government administrations that wanted him killed. I think he sealed that deal when he had hardworking people's ownership of property taken away, which caused a massive Cuban exile to Miami and New Jersey (Fidel Castro told me that everyone could have stayed where they were living if they chose to do so), as well as the execution of certain others, after he took power. Since his brother took over, Castro's top people were pushed aside, like Vice President Carlos Lage, Felipe Roque, who was foreign minister, and even Chomi, who retired from the secretariat of the Council of States, according to Marc Frank's book.

Fidel's brother put a new system in place. His people and his family have assumed many operational duties, as Raul seems to control politics, most business, and the military. The great Cuban culture, *siete anos*, and mojitos, live on to this day. However, the cartel system has not changed. Fidel's brother and family control the island through business, military, and politics, although officially at least Raul has recently stepped down politically. The Cuban market is still a strong, viable market for poultry and other agriculture-related products worth hundreds of millions in trade to the Cuban cartel nation. However, systematic problems continue to exist with the Socialist economy, including food and other essential shortages that have severely increased during Covid-19. This has led to uprisings across the island because the island is broke, there are shortages of essential medicine and food and "Havana [is] exporting doctors" for profit instead of having them stay home focused on the internal population. Cuba is also refusing international aid workers, according to Mary Anastasia O'Grady's *Wall Street Journal* op-ed "Behind Cuba's Covid Uprising."[7] Meanwhile, the regime points to the US travel restrictions, restrictions on family remittances, and the US overall embargo. A crackdown emerges again. We shall see what happens next.

CHAPTER FIVE

Early Years Training Ground and Tough Lessons Learned

Early Training
From Express Money to $1.2B MoneyGram

In 1986, I graduated from college and ran for state representative. I knocked on over twenty-five thousand doors and dropped off literature sometimes two and three times a day. I ran an organization raising $35,000 for the political campaign and attained a 39% share of the total vote. I pivoted and earned my stripes in the early corporate days fighting to gain market share from Western Union in the money transfer business by going after their agents to set up a competitive market for Citicorp, with goals to expand to other products and services.

Every six months, the bottom 20% seemed to get cut or quit nationally. I started with six account executives in New England. When I left, I was the only one remaining after working up to seven days per week, achieving agent distribution and initial and recurring revenue. After about eighteen months of success in setting up the business, Western Union sued Citicorp to put them out of business.

In Chapter Three of *Principles of Cartel Disruption*, I discuss the legal game. Scorch and burn is a legal strategy, and Western Union used it effectively. Citicorp Express Money disbanded after the legal battle. When the layoff occurred, I was part of the group that got paid double to stay on to shut things down since I was a top performer.

Meanwhile, American Express saw the great value proposition opportunity as noted in Chapter One of *Principles of Cartel Disruption*. Citicorp Express Money had tested and had agents set up across the country. They leveraged the cost of the network's setup and the opportunity in money transfer and cherry-picked the best account executives for its new MoneyGram service. I received an offer to work with MoneyGram, which scaled to a $1.2B business through operational excellence. I chose to go to business school at NYU Stern and worked for Chase Credit Card Marketing. I chose not to join American Express and didn't pick up Express Money's bones to convert them to MoneyGram's distribution and revenue.

The American Express division executive who gave me the offer was furious, as all other top Citi executives accepted them, which set up a national organization to accelerate growth. We had some outstanding accounts in

New England and the Boston-ADI market. And look what they did. Fantastic achievement, boys and girls.

Evening and Weekend Gigs

In the evening and on the weekends, I helped Andrew Natsios and Andy Card with Vice President H. W. Bush's campaign in Massachusetts and New Hampshire. We had more success than my run for state representative. I also paid my societal dues in Lexington, Mass., through town meetings, coaching football for the longest-serving high school head football coach in history, Bill Tighe at Lexington High School, and recruiting athletes for Tufts University.

I learned quite a bit during that period about marketing, sales, demographics, interest groups, and networking from this experience. It culminated with an exciting end to my political career at the 1988 Republican National Convention as a floor rally coordinator and alternate delegate. With Bush's opponent, Governor Michael S. Dukakis, being from Massachusetts, we had quite a bit of national media attention and interviews. I got to know the media quite well during those three days. It gave me practice with TV, radio, and print interviews. For the record, President H. W. Bush was tops in his league in terms of acumen, remembering names, and graciousness on every occasion I interacted with him while vice president and president. He also was kind enough to endorse my candidacy for state representative.

NYU Stern School of Business and Practical Education

At Stern, we had great positive innovation and acceleration taught and learned from former Kellogg executive Mike Darling. I learned the importance of investing capital on your brand launch, focusing on cash flow, and other lessons to drive your value proposition's success through test and acceleration, shown in both Chapter One on value proposition and Chapter Eight of *Principles of Cartel Disruption*, "Using Operational Metrics to Guide Your Test Marketing and Early Stage Milestones." More than anything, Mike Darling gave me confidence that I could succeed, as I seemed to grasp new products and new ventures better than most in the class.

Many other practical professors worked during the day and taught or gave seminars at night, such as Professor David Poltrack. In his day job, he was a senior executive at CBS in charge of market and advertising research and program testing and measurement. Former FED chairman Paul Volcker taught monetary policy. Professor W. Edwards Deming taught a legendary continuous quality improvement model and process excellence.

My favorite seminar was a behavioral lesson. A former alleged inside trader spoke to us after he got out of jail. The gentleman spent one hour apologizing for his behavior. When he finished, I raised my hand and asked him directly, "If you did not get caught, what would you be doing right now?" The man looked down at his watch, smiled, and said, "It's 4:30 p.m. I need to send a wire to Switzerland."

I learned the art of having experts from NYU Stern, some of which ended up on my board. I was able to get through school with John Hampton supporting me with quantitative matters, Lisa Fraser with qualitative matters, and Jeff Sirkin on real estate. Later, Lisa joined John and became key advisors on my board at Radlo Foods.

I had fun on business school projects that matriculated to a peculiar local pub, McSorley's, or other fine establishments from Greenwich Village down to Wall Street, adding in future consumer product experts Valerie Smith and Rob Sheckman; Sustainable Growth, finance, and Vanilla King George Fraise; and the Princeton boxer who Mike Tyson could never put down, now Professor Henry "Hank" Milligan. After graduating, I have gone back from time to time to give seminars and lectures.

While at NYU, I spent some time working at Chase Credit Card Marketing. Chase Marketing was exceedingly diverse, with a vast majority of the positions held by women. Lois Deming, former Colgate and now KFI-affiliated executive, led the acquisitions department. Lois married into the Kostelanetz-Deming side of the family to my second cousin Vlad, whose family came over from the old Soviet Union. She could not hire me directly but told me where I should send my resume. A few months later, I got a call and was picked up by the only old-school "manly man" unit over at Chase Credit Card Marketing, headed by Dave Hill, Ken Kraetzer, and Steve Eulie. They liked my Citicorp, NYU, and college athlete experience.

Chase was incubating and accelerating credit card insurance programs such as triple-digit growth Credit Life. It was the most net contribution income per employee that I had been involved in. We solicited existing Chase credit card customers with direct "snail mail" and by telephone. After seeing a call center operated, I nearly died on a puddle jumper airplane in a lightning storm coming back to Omaha, Nebraska. Ken to this day runs successful marketing programs as a supplier to Visa and has a great side gig giving back by running marketing promotions and programs to support West Point and Army football.

Effective Education

I am a big proponent of higher education that integrates the real world into its curriculum. My son, Ben, had an outstanding education at Northeastern through the cooperative education program. My daughter, Jess, integrated real-world experience at the BU College of Communication with internships. Currently, Dean Kevin Oye, Chris Swan, Professors Jack Derby (Former Chair of the Derby Entrepreneurship Center), and Tina Weber weave all things practical at my undergraduate alma mater, Tufts University, in the Gordon Institute of Innovation & Management, School of Engineering, and now the Derby Entrepreneurship Center. Jack Derby calls it "content in context" on my August 2021 ForbesBooks Radio podcast. Meanwhile, my lead NYU Stern mentor, Mike Darling, has moved back to Canada and is still giving it hell at Queen's College, designing and running programs. Also, I work with Bob Gough at the University of New Hampshire. To this day, I speak, lecture, coach, and provide seminars for students and corporate associations.

I also enjoy reaching a broader audience now with my second book and the ongoing podcast of "Sustainable Leadership and Disruptive Growth," partnered with ForbesBooks Radio, as noted above. We are transforming a safer, new, and better world with the best of the best sharing lessons for great young minds.

On a related note, I also continue to give back to support athletics and innovative growth at Tufts University. There is no better teacher of leadership, teamwork, processes, incremental improvement, and discipline than athletics. Therefore, I believe that athletics are as equally important as academics.

My daughter, Jess, is pictured below in Photo 5.A. leading her team on the water. As a former high school club and college rower and coach, Jess shares the same opinion. She used her international rowing and athletic network exceedingly effectively to advance and grind.

Leadership, teamwork, and gender equality are just how it is in the rowing world. There are great opportunities for young, hard-working athletes and former athletes, female or male when it comes to athletics. The picture in Photo 5.B. is the senior class football survivors after a mammoth 10-0 shutout Amherst College in 1985, disrupting their multiyear winning streak. This group produced a US Navy nuclear submarine commodore, a world-renowned orthopedic surgeon, the head of the New England Organized Crime Strike Force, international general counsel to a top worldwide company, an ADA in Brooklyn, a worldwide prestigious litigator, an international pilot, a Hollywood comedian, top corporate salespeople, top engineering management, and some with extreme success in business, along with me, jersey number sixty in the picture. Most importantly, we and the greater athletic and fraternal community have been there to help students with informational interviews and actual positions, increasing numbers year after year. We pass the culture and tradition of giving down and support Tufts to become the top innovative academic and athletic university.

Our spirited group, working with former athletes and friends of the university, replaced the former WWII military barracks seen in this picture with outstanding brick-and-mortar facilities, and we continue to upgrade. It's in our blood and culture. Principle 11 in *Principles of Cartel Disruption* is more than just a principle; it's at the core of who we are and what we do.

EXHIBIT 5.A. *Jess stroking (right behind #24). Her team doesn't know she's networking and developing a life-long positive growth mindset and competitive execution toughness.*

EXHIBIT 5.B. *This Successful Band (and many more of us) that Chooses to Give Back with Time, Talents, Contacts, and Money.*

Puerto Rican Chicken and Egg Cartel Action

In 1991, I fought the local egg producer cartel in Puerto Rico. The cartel worked to develop local Puerto Rican laws that effectively outlawed the sale of eggs in dozen packages and all eggs from the United States. Similar legislation was put forth on poultry as well. As noted in Chapter Three of *Principles of Cartel Disruption*, we learned and understood the basic legal game. We filed a lawsuit against the secretary of Agriculture in Puerto Rico for not allowing us to sell eggs in dozen packages and for violating the commerce clause and the supremacy clause of the Constitution after the product was held up at the port. We won a temporary restraining order, attained a permanent injunction, and won the case. These events allowed us to grow our market share. We beat the cartel in court due to Federal Judge Pérez-Giménez's rulings, and the local producer cartel in Puerto Rico was pretty pissed.

Leading up to this, we got frantic calls from customers that the laws were changing and that all US products would not be allowed into Puerto Rico anymore. Fortunately, my one semester of constitutional law in college helped, along with the best legal minds in the United States and Puerto Rico. I warned the lead producer on the island that if they went for our throat, we would file and not only go after maintaining our ability to ship non-carton eggs, but we would start shipping eggs in dozen cartons, which were banned at the time. He and his local producer cartel associates felt strongly about their position.

The laws changed with the local agriculture secretary's blessing to put the screws to US mainland producers, distributors, and marketing exporters to eliminate their local competition and increase their cash flow. They threatened us with the total extinction of selling products. To me, this was a call to war, which means get the best lawyers you can and sue! Attain restraining orders, permanent injunctions, and increase our cash flow. Crisis is an opportunity!

My dad was an esteemed WWII veteran. He was a liberator who served under George S. Patton in the humble but esteemed 395th. His unit was awarded the Presidential Unit Citation for heroism along with several battle stars, and he spent the rest of his days dealing with PTSD. My dad, Jack, lived through the most challenging parts of the European theatre and survived, which to him was all that mattered. We didn't discuss his citations or awards while he was alive. Previously, he said he learned toughness because of necessity, as he had to fight his way to school growing up in Boston. Dad used to say, "If they come after you, hit them as hard as you can and make sure they know that they have been in a fight. Make them respect you win or lose."

Fortunately, I organized a coalition of my customers and some suppliers to get some seed money and hire attorneys to fight it. On the US side, we had esteemed Washington attorneys Phil Olsson and David Durkin of Olsson, Frank, and Weeda (later OFW law). In Puerto Rico, we had Harvey Nachman and Horacio Figueroa Matos, outstanding attorneys with impeccable reputations.

Harvey was related to a neighbor whose kids I watched over growing up. One meeting, I Socratically questioned him, and he broke the power frame when he said, "Don't Jew me, Radlo," which caught me off guard. In Chapter Two of *Principles of Cartel Disruption*, I discuss the power frame technique when pitching an idea or business proposal. Harvey was always at the top of his game and could mix excitement, humor, toughness, and intellect. He continued by saying, "My mother used to do that to me just like you are doing now, and that's why I moved to Puerto Rico!" Rafi Vélez, who worked for us, and distributors Tito Rodriguez and Jorge Meyandia have all never let me forget that and thought it was the best comeback that they had ever heard. I paused before serially questioning Harvey again.

We had the full support of the lawsuit from the United Egg Producers (UEP).

Senior management Al Pope, Ken Klippen, and Gene Gregory all testified at different times. The United States Department of Agriculture (USDA) also testified, along with a local group representing poultry and egg importers in Puerto Rico, the Puerto Rican Meat Institute, which represented distributors. You can handle sustainable leadership and diplomacy in one instance while disrupting another situation.

These fights went on for several years, and we prevailed every time while doubling our business as we started shipping carton eggs! What did President Gerald Ford say? "Hail to the Constitution!" And hail to the commerce and supremacy clause. Thank you, undergraduate professor of constitutional law, Marilyn Glater at Tufts University, and thank you to classmates and Harvard Law School-bound Anthony "Mooch" Scaramucci and Kevin "Clots" Cloherty for recommending her course over beers with Rick "Dickie" Lerner! For several years, this case was apparently on the bar exam.

Toughness Learned the Hard Way—Coldcock Punching a Shipping Cartel

In 1994, I learned the most significant learning lesson of my life, and it was the cornerstone of my future success. At our company, we had a business that leased refrigerated containers. We leased to an affiliate of a Puerto Rican carrier of my associate Mike Shea, president of Sea-Barge. The sister affiliate company was called Sea-Xpress, and they shipped to the Bahamas. It was for sale and seemed like an easy fix. We would get the correct equipment and sail out of Fort Lauderdale instead of Miami. This change would cut costs and maximize orders in covering Nassau and Freeport. The projections looked very promising.

Long-time veterans Dewey Parker, who went to school with Burt Reynolds and was a great host of parties on the water near Coral Gables, and Vic Otero, a former New Yorker, ran the business. With the right formula, success seemed imminent. We purchased the company from Henry van der Kwast, from the Dutch island Curaçao, with his finance guy, Ken Sousa. Right before the deal closed, Crowley Maritime shot in and started shipping to the Bahamas. We should have walked and taken the losses in container revenue that we would have sustained if we pulled away from the deal. However, we didn't. I had not learned the first strategic planning trap from *Principles of Cartel Disruption*. In Chapter Four, I talk about the trap of failing to recognize and understand events and changing conditions in the competitive marketplace, but that's what I did.

I took a loan, purchased the business, executed the plan, and leased a new equipment fleet. Operationally it was a success. However, we went after Tropical Shipping's largest customer while Crowley, the new entrant, kept eroding our business. It was deadly. The boys that were in a shipping conference, which is a legal entity that allows price and related discussions, had enough of SeaXpress.

After we successfully attained Tropical Shipping's largest customer, they retaliated and lowered their rates to $20 per shipment in some cases, plus landing and other fees. We did not have the capital to fight them. We had leases that would sink our entire business interest. We were able to sell it under duress to Harry Bresky, a seaboard Marine, through their marine affiliate. John Lynch was the head of the shipping business, and Bruce Brecheisen was the CFO of the subsidiary company.

We got out of the lease liabilities but lost about $1.3M and had allocated $900,000 in cash. The situation created the threat of bankruptcy. It was an absolute disaster, and everyone sued us. I got a harsh lesson in the basic legal game and learned the hard way about law and business. Holland & Knight in Miami, including Raul Cosio, Jose Casal, and Juan Enjamio, bailed our asses out. They represented us, and we settled with creditors the best we could. We had all types of commercial litigation stacked against us.

We tried to sue the company that sold us the business, but their attorney, Tim Armstrong, gave me a lesson on the law. He fought everything along the way. He fought service, forum non conveniens, every answer, and every discovery. When I was through with SeaXpress and Tim Armstrong's litigation, I had filled legal education gaps from my one semester of business law in graduate school.

I received a real-life education on quashing service, fraud in the inducement, breach of fiduciary duties, unfair business practices, negligent misrepresentations, breach of contract, tortious interference, employment contract issues, letter of intent contract issues, antitrust violations. I felt that every form and facet of the law was involved in the SeaXpress clusterf-ck. It was a million-dollar pragmatic legal education.

After it was over, I received a call from an intermediary letting me know the shipping cartel "hit" allegedly may have been coordinated. They wanted to let me know how much they appreciated my shipping business over the years as a poultry and egg exporter and to ensure that they would treat us right as a customer but not as a competitor.

This situation made me a seasoned and tough business executive. I developed steadfast principles in business. I developed eyes in the back of my head, which came in handy in dealing with "Bad Boy" Jack DeCoster and his sidekick "Duke" Goranites, venture capitalists, investment bankers, and the review of deals and acquisitions. My skills also helped me grow organically and inorganically through acquisition in agriculture, consumer products, biotech, entertainment, tech, real estate, and more, but I was done with shipping!

This horrifically bad deal led me to learn an uncanny ability to find a path to a profitable sea change of growth and the ability to envision synergistic partnerships, alliances, and M and A targets while navigating the minefields.

In the end, we lost a lot of money but averted total failure to fight another day. My related container business was gone. I had a big loan to pay back, and the debtors deservedly were pissed at me for being a dumbass and coldcocking a shipping cartel.

In those days, I lived on meager savings just as my son, Ben, was coming into the world. In any event, it was a sobering time. I thought that I was done with disrupting entrepreneurial America and was starting to network back to my friends near Wall Street in New York for a resurrection. However, with a large amount of debt and lots of hard work after learning from my mistakes, I was able to turn things around into great success.

The bigger your mistakes, the harder you will fall. But there is a gift in the lesson. The bigger the challenge, the more you learn. With grit, you can overcome your missteps. I shifted to building other businesses, doubling the revenue of a commodity business and then selling parts of it to pay the debt I owed. The skills from the disaster were starting to pay off in a big way, positioning me for the future.

CHAPTER SIX

Inside Secret Look at Attaining Sustainable Excellence in the Tough Egg and Food Industry: Wars between Animal Rights Groups and Agriculture and the

Incubation of Cage Free Nation.

In Chapter One of *Principles of Cartel Disruption*, "Accelerate and Maximize Performance," I detail how I founded Radlo Foods in 1998 to focus on growth in the egg and food business with healthy, sustainable nutrition and also to increase nutraceutical inputs and organic and humane foods. It was a successor business to Radlo Brothers Markets that my grandfather Mark started in 1916 with his brothers. Their company began in Quincy Market in Boston, delivering food with a horse and a cart, and my WWII-GI dad, Jack Radlo, grew Brown Eggs Fresh from New England.

In 1998, when we started Radlo Foods, we had a small commodity-based business of $10M, more or less, with very low margins. Since that very humble start, we had a run of consistent double- and triple-digit growth over that period. We grew revenue by 10X and a 30X increase in enterprise value, incubating, and accelerating products with brands like Eggland's Best, Born Free, and Farmer's Best with people, process, and strategy with a sustainable focus at home and low-cost food shipped abroad. These precursors tied into the great business that we developed in Cuba along with an outstanding biotech business.

My industry partners also did exceedingly well from innovative disruption and acceleration. The specialty egg and related food business boomed into the billions in sales, focusing on a small piece of a large market chock full of growth trends. It took seven days per week and a twenty-three-hour operation per day to manage this rocket ship of growth, which had plenty of challenges and setbacks. Still, in the end, it was one heck of a fun ride focused on respect for people and measurable incremental improvement.

The egg industry has spent millions of dollars successfully defending antitrust allegations with defense verdicts relating to increasing space to address humane concerns. They deserve the right to be an association. They are benevolent in that they feed the poor with low-cost food and a concerted industry effort to give free eggs to food banks from coast to coast throughout the year.

Through Covid-19 in 2020 and 2021, the egg industry and food industry as a whole faced unprecedented hardship. In the face of the pandemic, extraordinary efforts were made to fill the increased retail demand and reroute different specification eggs from the food service channels to the grocery shelves. Still, they continued their unwavering support of local food pantries and food banks.

There have been some price gouging complaints by states resulting from pandemic-related market forces. Urner Barry has been independently quoting the egg and other food protein markets for over a century. At the beginning of the pandemic, it may have been beyond the control of producers trying to meet orders and keep their essential employees safe and healthy. Prices retreated later in the year with an oversupply and lack of food service business. The egg and related food business is a tough business that involves live animals, perishable commodities, and high seasonal spikes in demand. It also runs seven days per week, and operations run close to twenty-four hours per day. This business is challenging in normal circumstances. Below is a slice of life of how we in the industry handled a challenging turnaround situation.

Brown Egg New England World and Lean Process Operational Excellence and Culture Change: (See Chapters Four through Seven in *Principles for Cartel Disruption*)

Lean Process Excellence in Action: Maine Culture Turnaround

To expand production to handle increased business due to a consumer boycott of a "bad boy" in the egg industry, we tackled a culture turnaround in individual facilities in Maine. Austin "Jack" DeCoster was an egg mogul. News reports alleged he was involved with facilities that sickened up to fifty-six thousand people in the Midwest. He served jail time for his role in the alleged sickness. The facilities we acquired were next door to DeCoster's remaining operation in Maine. We had purchased and leased the facilities about a decade before the issue occurred in the Midwest. Several problems involving worker safety, wastewater treatment, food safety, and operational excellence were present.

We added a former engine room military and egg industry veteran named Tom Shea to the team to change the culture. He was famous for working tirelessly, and he treated problems as opportunities. He led operational management and brought diversity and inclusivity objectives to the operation.

We brought in an exceptional operational and technical business executive, Scott Burns, from Egg Fusion to tackle food safety and technological initiatives.

The team was the best in the industry. It fought daily in the toughest of environments, considering the dysfunctional environment we were competing with next door. Eventually, we promoted Gay Smith to be the first woman to run a processing and production operation in Maine.

In our executive conference, we identified several areas to reduce waste and create variation improvement. The most significant area of improvement was how to handle the eggs. Inexperienced handlers routinely were not removing enough imperfections in eggs. This challenge caused quality issues with our customers, even after passing USDA inspection. As a quality-focused organization, we had higher expectations than the USDA.

Our initiative was to train our personnel better. The same was true with OSHA (Occupational Safety and Health Administration) safety issues. We developed a committee of employees that met regularly to discuss the related challenges. We created a strong relationship with the aid of expert OSHA consultant Deb Roy, OSHA Operational Director Sam Kondrup, and the area head, Bill Freeman.

In the early 2000s, the first OSHA inspection that made newspaper headlines revealed we had received no fines. The inspection was important because our neighbor DeCoster had received millions of dollars in fines, which caused him to lose most of his business due to a consumer boycott.

The same was true for wastewater treatment and nitrate runoff. We had John Engel of Engel Environmental do inspections to determine the nitrate runoff level. We diligently took the time to ensure that our wastewater treatment was in line with the Maine Department of Environmental Protection (DEP) and the US Environmental Protection Agency (EPA). We also focused on water quality for the workers and ensured testing regularly. This process took place after DeCoster received a consent order for wastewater treatment, or lack thereof.

We worked with Dr. Mike Opitz, State Veterinarian Don Hoenig, Assistant State Veterinarian Beth McEvoy, and Deputy Agriculture Commissioner Ned Porter to ensure we were following the food safety requirements of the Maine Salmonella Enteritidis Risk Reduction Program. We depopulated the production facility so we could adequately fill the mouse holes. Mice were carriers of *Salmonella enteritidis*. After baiting, we put forth appropriate cleaning. We eradicated *Salmonella enteritidis* with a lot of work. Scott Burns was crucial in implementing a comprehensive food safety plan, including Safe Quality Food (SQF) inspections.

Scott and Tom said that they couldn't do their jobs because of the proximity of all of the industry's facilities in Maine. In his aircraft carrier engine room crisis voice, Tom Shea added appropriate color to the situation. New Jersey native Scott Burns characterized the issue stemming from DeCoster's facilities as the "decision-making of madmen," which was reported in September 2010 by New England Cable News.

Early on, Scott and Tom attempted to work without the state to remedy the biosecurity problems. They confronted their management at a meeting. They were concerned that the biosecurity situation could result in jail time for the management team if not rectified. According to Scott, one of DeCoster's senior managers lifted his leg to show an ankle bracelet he was wearing for an alleged unrelated past transgression. The man smiled and said, "The worst that they could do to me is add more time on my ankle bracelet."

We enlisted the state with the help of Bill Bell of the New England Brown Egg Council and industry veterans Julia and John Lough at the nearby Dorothy Egg Farms. I was president of the council, and Bill was executive director. We applied political pressure. It was a complicated task to eradicate salmonella from farms in Maine. We did it and passed the FDA inspection in 2010. Although it takes strong leadership to implement process improvement and excellence, regardless of the obstacles, with proper guidance and a great team, it can and will happen!

PHOTO 6.A.

Bill Bell is pictured with me at a United Egg Producer meeting in Washington with newlyweds Mr. and Mrs. Peter DeCoster ("Bad Boy" Jack's son and daughter-in-law. I can verify Peter is very tough, strong, and direct. He was usually in Maine to run "cleanup," like when the roof caved in on our leased plant or other significant issues like food safety compliance matters with the state of Maine regulatory authorities).

Caged to Cage Free

We struck a deal in 2004 to change the first barn in the United States from caged to cage-free laying hens on Dorothy's Egg Farm in Winthrop, Maine, in cooperation with John and Julia Lough. It was a tremendous endorsement of the movement we had started with products from Pennsylvania and Ohio. We worked with Larry Shirk and Jim Adams at Wenger Feeds in PA and later Paul Kalmbach, as well as CBI, in Ohio, along with Paul and Mark Sauder of

Sauder's Eggs in PA. Ryan Miller of Farmers Hen House in Ohio, Jesse and Gerry LaFlamme of Pete and Gerry's/Nellie's were all partners in this progress. Others that joined the march towards a Cage Free nation were Organic Front, Steve Herbruck and family in Michigan, Mike Sencer and Tim Luberski of Hidden Villa, and later Greg Hinton and Marcus Rust from Rose Acre Farms.

HSUS Interaction

I met Washington attorney Phil Olsson of OFW Law in the early 2000s with the Humane Society of the United States (HSUS). Until this time, the humane groups were characterized unfavorably at times because some would break into labs, free mice, and subject the public to health and wellness issues. I observed the inner workings of a group of executives collaborating for animal rights and welfare. They had a working group of associations that earned their organizations quite a bit of money and preached a social mission. The unofficial leadership was coordinated within the HSUS through intense collaboration.

The Agriculture Industry Successfully Positioned the Animal Rights Groups as Radicals

The HSUS had an impeccable reputation in Washington. Past president and CEO Wayne Pacelle and his top operating executive, Michael Markarian, worked with his team, including Minyan Park, Paul Shapiro, and later Josh Balk, who ran the factory farm campaign. They were hardcore vegans but very practical and considered animal rights activists, rather than an animal welfare group that certified our products with Certified Humane labels like Adele Douglass's group, and American Humane, which was Kathi Brock and Tim Amlaw's group.

Adele Douglass, at first, was considered an enemy of the allied industry along with the HSUS, but that changed when we started marketing humane products in the allied industry and started to grab market share with third-party certification. The HSUS blessed us as acceptable. Then I persuaded Steve Herbruck, the president and owner of Herbruck's Poultry Ranch in Michigan, a major United Egg and organic producer, to pack "Certified Humane" for Radlo Foods. He agreed, and overnight Adele Douglass's organization became a mainstream-accepted animal welfare organization by the industry. She was thrilled.

When we met with Wayne and Paul at dinner, we ate at a vegan restaurant in Washington. We had a comprehensive, thoughtful discussion. We looked at what was good in both of us before discussing any differences of opinion. The HSUS was looking for incremental improvement in animal welfare conditions. We were willing to continue the discussion and meet partway. Radlo Foods was the first major producer and marketer in agriculture to meet with them, and they appreciated the overture.

When we met the HSUS in their offices near Washington in 2006, Wayne and Paul were there along with Mike Markarian, Minyan Park, and others. I brought the marketing group headed by Mark Shuster and Joan Leroy. The HSUS wanted to know what the market for cage-free would be and the prospects for moving towards more humane treatment of laying hens and other farm animals. We were questioned about what was practical. I outlined this in Chapter One of *Principles of Cartel Disruption* in terms of the value proposition for the socially progressive customer base.

I told them that if on a consumer-choice basis, cage-free eggs ended up on the shelf of supermarkets with 100% all category volume (ACV), we projected 3–5% of the product sold would be at least cage-free. One hundred percent ACV meant that 100% of supermarkets and retail outlets carried the product. This projection included free-range and organic within three to five years. Within ten years, there would be a commitment towards either colony group housing or cage-free. And if you made vegan products that did not taste like crap, perhaps meat eaters may buy them based upon taste, along with health reasons, as long as the price was in the ballpark.

Pacelle, Markarian, and Park looked shocked, while Shapiro, a cartel disrupter himself, smiled and knew that it could happen. Shapiro had targeted plans inside the organization to make it happen. I gave him the independent validation that there would be production to fill the consumer orders of cage-free and longer-term alternative protein. This meeting cemented my relationship with Wayne, Paul, and the Humane Society of the United States.

Soon after Josh Balk joined the crew, meanwhile, I believed with the reduction of chickens in cages the egg industry couldn't screw it up, and any investment in equipment would be more than offset by increased profits from the change to fewer birds per square foot. This situation was a win-win for all. Savvy class-action attorneys saw that too and later put a different spin on it.

We realized that they were already shedding light on production practices through undercover videos either directly or in contact with other animal rights organizations that were a bit more aggressive, such as Mercy for Animals. Paul Shapiro had started Compassion Over Killing several years earlier. Given his ability to collect video footage and do media exposés, Shapiro had real power to bring about change.

Everything was done with the HSUS in the diplomatic and politically correct way with retailers. The HSUS always started with an 8.5 x 11-inch sheet of paper and said, "This is how much space a hen has for her life." They wanted to move to cage-free systems. Retailers would have an opportunity to meet them halfway by putting products on the cage-free shelf. If they did not, there would be a compelling force to have them change all of their eggs to cage-free.

Shapiro would work to tie the production practices of their suppliers that were under investigation to the product that was sold by the chains. They would construct elaborate guerilla marketing campaigns by having their base supporters reach out and contact supermarkets or others targeted for change. This practice carried over to food service.

For the most part, producers and marketers of cage-free products were not attacked directly by the HSUS. The policy of the HSUS was to let the retailers know exactly where the cards were being played. Then, when they did not meet them halfway, the "Prince of Darkness," as allied agriculture referred to Shapiro, would whack them hard, which would be an exposé tying cruelty to their business. I observed it happen repeatedly. Their creativity in this disruption endeavor from the sidelines was legendary.

Many producers prominently had food service businesses or were independent farmers who felt that no one would dictate to them. They also had a price edge on the UEP-certified producers, as those that did not shift practices could offer a lower cost or make more profit, as they were getting more birds per cage.

UEP leaders were frustrated with members that were significant producers that would not comply. In public meetings, Gene would look at me and say, "Some producers have decided that they want to sit down and break bread with the enemy to market cage-free. We believe in free choice, but we certainly don't welcome this treasonous conduct." It felt as though he was looking at me like I was Benedict Arnold.

Gene played up the common enemy approach that was a typical tactic in the specialty egg category leadership and outside disruption. We are innovators and bell ringers. We are used to running differently than the allied industry, which gives us a competitive edge. We have a fast-growing segment of a large category and, in this case, for animal welfare and consumer choice, so we did not feel that we were out of line in this regard.

We ran the other way with commodity brown eggs in New England but organized the local industry in that regard. Frankly, I saw this as another free-market edge to get ahead of the curve. However, we played mainstream ball and exported billions of eggs overseas, including to Canada, Puerto Rico, Cuba, Hong Kong, Dubai, and elsewhere from many of the UEP members. As head of the New England Brown Egg Council, we aligned with industry-government relations in Washington and New England.

I also served on the American Egg Board, with an appointment from the US secretary of Agriculture and served as a board member of the United States Poultry and Egg Export Council, which was the export arm of the poultry (chicken, turkey, and duck), egg, and egg product industry. We were treated with genuine respect. The agriculture industry is a "clubby" but at times very cutthroat place. As an example, supermarket "slotting" in the egg industry started early in the last third of the twentieth century when long-time industry sales veteran Fred Hersey, who had the extra product, talked a New England supermarket buyer into taking money "above the table" for additional product sold into the stores—an ingenious move at the time to get rid of extra products that incubated and accelerated into a national profit center for retailers.

After the meetings were over, I would get a call from the egg industry's "Deep Throat," as they used to refer to that anonymous FBI agent during the Nixonian Watergate days. The egg industry's "Deep Throat" would make a plea that I pass on to the HSUS not to attack UEP-certified producers. Some may have interpreted that as a nice way of saying "whack" the other producers so they fall into line with the UEP program. Given the HSUS's plan to upgrade the industry, this was one of the only things that they and the UEP had an agreement on. There was no direct communication for plausible deniability.

The HSUS whacked many producers. Some lost pretty sizable retail, big box, and food service accounts from undercover video footage if the producers could not denounce the footage as a setup. It was harder for non-UEP producers to meet the requirement because the farms didn't meet base industry standards. Some producers later used the USDA verification program so that some of their flocks could meet standards while others would not.

The UEP certification program required producers to have all of their birds in the program. In fairness to producers that provided products to the food service and ingredient customers, they would lose a significant share of business and profitability because of the increased costs. There were holdouts, as not every customer cared what type of eggs they received.

United Egg Producers: No Good Deed Goes Unpunished

Trying to get ahead of the humane curve, as early as the 1990s the UEP started planning, working, and executing their animal welfare program. The HSUS attacked the UEP Certified program. It was also the focal point of antitrust issues of collective producer attempts to raise prices through animal welfare by reducing chickens in a cage and an export program where producers would sell products overseas with the direct purpose of increasing the market. They believed it was legal under the Capper-Volstead antitrust exemption. The legal team that advised the UEP and the producers thought these actions were acceptable, but the class action 25–35% contingency commission of the legal folks who sued disagreed. The egg industry companies involved with this program have paid tens of millions of dollars in legal fees and hundreds of millions of dollars in settlement costs. The loss was painful but a cost of doing business in the egg industry.

Some agricultural producers have a cartel mentality that was reinforced through the years by attorneys. Attorneys earned quite a bit of money from preaching the producer's legal argument for being exempt from antitrust lawsuits due to Capper-Volstead protection allowing producers to discuss prices. Billable-hour lawyers were available during official UEP meetings to discuss potential lawsuits, settlements, rationale, and the endless legal arguments espoused. It went on and on and on.

Antitrust arguments were a legal opportunity for class action and certain customers to grab some bucks from the producers on a reduced birdcage allegation to drive market prices higher. This situation wasn't exactly fair, as the producers absorbed high costs by taking birds out of cages with more facilities. As noted above, the other major antitrust allegation issue was exporting eggs offshore to increase the market on a concerted, organized basis. This action was at best a misunderstanding because as producers worked together on the belief that they were exempt from antitrust laws, the effects of taking birds out of cages in a rapid manner without resupply would undeniably raise the market, even if it was short term.

A UEP senior producer stated to me, "David, the producers can't screw it up by cheating, even if they wanted to." The rules guard against the likelihood that producers may try to cheat by adding birds back to an existing flock, called "backfilling," or grow faster with fewer birds in a cage. Therefore, having fewer birds in a cage made for more stable markets from a supply-and-demand standpoint.

However, his good friend and senior national production leader at the time, Jerry Kil, disagreed and told me, "Those that were not participating in the program could flood the market and fill the void, and producers always overproduce in time. That's what they get up in the morning to do—produce! And produce they do!" There were other price enhancement practices that the egg producers believed were perfectly legal and within their rights to follow. They shipped containers of commodity eggs overseas to raise the commodity prices, which directly impacted short-term prices, especially during bad times for farmers when producers were losing money and prices were low. The banks and other financial lenders were bearing down.

The bird reduction claim made to increase prices was not exactly fair as most, if not all, chains and businesses that sued were aware of it up front. The industry was reacting under animal welfare pressure coming via the retailers and businesses from the humane groups.

In Chapter Three of *Principles of Cartel Disruption*, I discuss understanding the basic legal game: "Lawsuits are for lawyers." The boys and girls in the law firms cleaned up on both sides of the fight, whether they were defending the producers or getting a nice share of the settlements. However, they lost some money when they went to trial and lost.

One UEP producer disclosed in their financial statements that they paid a settlement, excluding legal fees, of $28M for one lawsuit and $80.8M for another. Some suit settlements reportedly paid $25M, $3M, $1.425M, and $500K. The ones that stayed the course and took it to trial flipped the coin of attorney Chris Kenney, former president of the Massachusetts Bar Association, as noted in Chapter Three of *Principles of Cartel Disruption.* The egg producers going to trial have won two defense verdicts and only had to pay legal fees and costs throughout the process and of course no judgments in those cases.

Antitrust attorneys representing members of a class-action lawsuit are suing other agricultural commodity groups for collusion, and this rooster says with confidence that the egg came before the chicken. However, we now know that the egg cases were warm-ups compared to the chicken cases. The Antitrust Division of the Justice Department has come forth as well. If convicted, that means possible jail time. With great legal counsel, jail time is generally avoided at all costs by firms if they can afford to write a big check and do a decent job begging for forgiveness. The settlements with the poultry industry have resulted in agreements that are not exactly "chicken feed" in size, with hundreds of millions of dollars in payments. Few are willing to put on attorney Chris Kenney's wedding ring and go to trial in consumer, wholesaler, and federal action. It isn't over. Not to leave the bacon out, there is a pork antitrust lawsuit, and one firm settled for $20M. The fish industry faces challenges as well. The class-action antitrust lawsuit business is a real niche in the litigating legal community, with the prospects of outrageous verdicts and a ridiculous amount of legal fees. It makes settling claims worthwhile, regardless of guilt or innocence, while avoiding jail and government action.

There are only a few dominant plaintiff antitrust legal firms, and at times they share risks and rewards to maximize cash flow and growth. Now, what does that sound like? Good thing the trial lawyers in America have a strong lobby in Congress so business is maintained and accelerated. God forbid they ever change the law so that the loser of a lawsuit must pay the legal fees to minimize lawsuits, like what happens in other countries. Tort reform? "HELL, NO!" say the legal boys and girls.

Back to the HSUS

Starting in the 2000s, the HSUS pushed hard for their vegan-rights agenda as part of their factory farming campaign led by Shapiro and Josh Balk in Washington. They had an office in the basement bunker of the HSUS with "battery cages" right over their desks in living color to see along with other confinement devices such as veal stalls and pork gestation crates. Shapiro and the HSUS coined the phrase "battery cages" because in the media they characterized the cages as the size of a car battery.

PHOTO 6.B. *Allied Egg Industry March on Washington, DC, circa 2010s. I am in the second row, two people from the left.*

The big producers that were susceptible to HSUS attacks were in the referendum states. An initiative petition could cause a ballot referendum pushing towards a mandated cage-free law and target the non-UEP-certified folks either in those states or nearby. The Farm Bureau lobbied heavily and at times allied with the agriculture industry to block initiatives. At the ballot box, people would vote their conscience or respond to the negative advertising of the HSUS. However, most people would vote with their wallets in the retail stores by buying the cheaper caged options. The HSUS did many polls and focus groups on attacking these issues.

I did have some meetings in a vegan restaurant in Georgetown with the HSUS once per year to discuss the issues. But I was still the diplomatic president of the New England Brown Egg Council, which was an advertising and promotional support and industry advocacy group. I testified at hearings in New Hampshire, Maine, and Massachusetts. We killed a "100% Cage-Free" bill in New Hampshire, and their lead representative also insulted and disrespected the chairman during the hearing. So it was dead to rights from the beginning.

In one of those Georgetown meetings, we jointly agreed to avoid a referendum in Maine by grandfathering existing systems but banning future veal crate gestation stalls and battery cages without a referendum. We called it the "Grandfather Compromise." The agreement was subject to us being able to convince legislators and work with allied agriculture. Maine is a practical place, and we were able to get allied agriculture, including the Maine Farm Bureau, to go along with it.

A similar deal was offered in California to allied industry according to Humane Society sources. The industry chose to go to the ballot with an initiative petition and millions spent on a consumer-choice campaign backed by the UEP and local groups. Pacelle worked in Hollywood for endorsements. The "Prince of Darkness," Paul Shapiro, allegedly may have worked on undercover videos during the campaign, especially from after Labor Day to election day.

The HSUS eliminated battery cages along with veal crates and gestation stalls in California by a landslide, and the egg industry not only lost the millions it had invested but had billions in future liabilities with increased cage costs going forward across the nation. All they had to do was eliminate veal crates, gestation stalls, and even grandfather in existing caged facilities to give time for farmers to allow the depreciation of existing facilities to run its course over the typical life cycle so they could survive.

Veal crates were suspect at best by taking baby male calves and tying them up for their lives in a veal hutch, rather than let them roam around free through the grass or inside in inclement conditions, so the meat would be more tender. Tom Shea, the former aircraft carrier engine room SVP of Production for our company, was not a shrinking violet. He never ate veal because of the treatment of the animal. Frankly, I have not eaten veal in decades since I learned about this treatment until American Humane and Certified Humane got involved with certifying. Veal produced with their logo to verify conditions is acceptable—nothing like an outside third party with a conscience to verify conditions.

The second practice was pork gestation stalls. The industry equipment manufacturers found a way to work around this process, but every producer did not use it. I believe this was a small concession as well. However, the pork farmers were not vertically integrated like the egg farmers and took the National Farm Bureau's "slippery slope" argument to lobby. In my opinion, they were selfish, aggressive, and not practical with these situations, especially in referendum states where voters could decide after seeing videos exposing the practices.

The New England Brown Egg Council represented the producers backed by the Maine Farm Bureau. In Maine, a deal with the HSUS ensured eliminating veal crates and gestation stalls for the future. Egg production was allowed to continue. However, another senior person in the humane groups bought an insurance policy and ordered a clandestine hit against a neighboring farmer, "Bad Boy" Austin "Jack" DeCoster through Mercy for Animals.

In this situation, DeCoster had four plants in Turner, Maine, but had two barn workers in the farm part of the facility where we purchased eggs. Dorothy Egg Farms was now operating it when we assigned the lease to them several years prior, as our focus was the new specialty and humane cage-free, free-range, and free-range organic. John and the Loughs did a better job dealing with Jack directly and with his lead enforcer Doucas "Duke" Goranites. The legal fights and costs with "Bad Boy" Jack were approximately over a million dollars.

When our senior leadership could not solve issues such as biosecurity with our esteemed neighbors, as their behavior directly affected our ability to operate, I would get a call for a sit down with "Bad Boy" Jack and Duke. This type of situation usually meant bringing in attorneys, or we had to get the state agriculture secretary's office to call an industry meeting in conjunction with the New England Brown Egg Council.

One time, we tried to settle an issue in person. Duke, a former football offensive lineman who outweighed me by quite a bit, could be intimidating and was exceedingly forceful. Being a former high school and college defensive lineman, albeit a bit undersized, and a coach whose specialty was to take on double teams and defend short-yardage situations, I understood the principle of leverage. Breaking the power frame is necessary, as noted in *Principles of Cartel Disruption* Chapter Two, where I discuss how to pitch an idea or opportunity.

In college, I had parking lot sessions with five-time All-Pro Buffalo Bills nose tackle Fred Smerlas. In summers before college football, we grappled outside of Joe Lavolli and the late Greg Kasabian's Olympia Gym in Woburn-Wakefield, MA. I ended up with a broken and very bloody nose, but I didn't know that these experiences would be helpful after college and for on-field football coaching.

However, I was wrong. I looked at Duke and, with my right thumb and index finger six inches apart near his neck, said, "I just want to thrust my hand under your chin, push upward around your neck, and squeeze." On many occasions when fights broke out, lawyers all jumped to their feet on both sides. In this situation, "Bad Boy" Jack said, "David, David, pleeease. I need Duke around.

You made your point."

Doing business with Jack and Duke was close to doing hand-to-hand combat. John Lough of Dorothy Egg Farms took over these facilities with our quality control to operate more effectively and efficiently with people, process, strategy, and sustainability. At first, I thought that John changed my original deal and had his own guys in the barns after taking over my previously acquired facilities. However, John had the same attitude that I had when I made the deal.

How could a couple of barn workers screw things up? There were so many fights with the other side that John prioritized which battles we needed to fight. It was an oversight on both our parts. Therefore, the deal that I made several years earlier when I assigned the facilities to John and Julia came back to haunt us. I traded millions of dollars of repairs to the facility where the roof had caved in a few weeks after taking it over. OSHA put the screws to DeCoster on the lease because we had to improve the conditions of the facilities to operate it properly.

The roof collapse was one of many lucky blessings. It occurred between 3:30 and 4:30 a.m., the only hour when no one worked in the production, processing, and load-out facility. There might have been serious injuries or a fatality if there were employees present. When telling this to my tough guy attorney, Alan Reisch, who worked with Kitt Sawitsky and Greg Getschman at Goulston & Storrs, he quipped, "Don't complain about the legal fees. They will be high on this one and continue to be high as we work through this and you continue to fight with these guys."

We agreed that they would pay for the fixes to the new plant we acquired at the time with the attorney's assistance. I never considered how one or two barn men could disrupt our business while DeCoster rehabilitated the place. As DeCoster used to say, "David, now chickens always come home to roost. Yessiree." Yes, indeed they do, "Bad Boy" Jack.

Mercy for Animals filed a complaint with the state of Maine. Unfortunately, many videos that leak can end up being a setup to foster an agenda. Our good friend Maine State Veterinarian Don Hoenig came in with his staff in white coats to survey humane conditions and found too many birds in some cages and fewer birds in others. They also codified Mercy for Animals' concerns with inhumane practices.

There was a video turned over to the state and press with footage showing the inappropriate handling of birds. This video may have been a setup. There is a humane way to cervically dislocate a chicken, and there is the way that was demonstrated in the video. The animal rights group had the situation set up and filed with the state. It was a media disaster for us, and the organized humane groups hit a grand slam. The factory farming campaign of the HSUS, the de facto humane association leader, although they jostle at times with

People for the Ethical Treatment of Animals (PETA), was usually at the hub of any hit, despite any plausible deniability nonsense that some may argue.

I sat there in Watertown, Mass., at our headquarters while operations head in Maine, Tom Shea, gave us an emergency "D-Day" email along with pictures of the state in white coats entering the facility on a raid and surprise inspection. I immediately ordered the de facto public relations guy for damage control. We pulled down to avoid a brand-tarnishing disaster. We quickly painted the sides of our trucks to cover anything that included our brands or name. I also mandated that all calls be forwarded to me until we hired O'Neill and Associates: Hugh Drummond, Andy Paven, and Ann Murphy along with Tom O'Neill. They did an excellent job of damage control. Hugh is the best in the business, and Ann Murphy is a consummate professional. Tom, a former lieutenant governor of Massachusetts and son of the late US House of Representatives Speaker "Tip" O'Neill, is the guru of damage control government relations in New England, with offices in Boston and Washington, DC.

Tom O'Neill and company were of great assistance a few years later when the industry had to deal with the media and an FDA inspection in Maine. Massachusetts Senator (then Congressman) Edward Markey called for one in a congressional hearing on the matter where "Bad Boy" Jack and his family had to testify. A large farmer who leased Iowa facilities from Jack chose not to participate in the congressional investigation, and his lawyers had him plead the fifth.

Generally, I felt sorry for the farmer getting dragged in like that. This situation occurred after a national egg recall. There was a congressional investigation into "Bad Boy" Jack's facilities in Iowa. There wasn't a food safety compliance protocol like there was in Maine. Therefore, there was no one in Iowa in government compliance with the flashlight, measuring stick, and hammer required to deal with "Bad Boy" Jack.

The FDA quickly brought all three to the situation after people started getting sick. The FDA followed the Iowa inspections to Maine, where the industry was operating under state of Maine compliance and protocols on food safety and our tireless work to raise the industry's bar. Immediately following Markey's request, the federal inspection in Maine came forth and took several weeks. It resulted in clean results for facilities handling quality assurance for our egg supply in cooperation with John and Julia Lough. I am delighted to give bonus awards for that!

No one understood why I hired Scott Burns to run food safety in Maine. He was a relentless Operational Excellence operator in all things people, process, strategy, and sustainability protocols, as noted in Chapters Four through Seven of *Principles of Cartel Disruption*. He worked with the legendary, late Tom Shea, John Stevens, and farmers John and Julia Lough. I got grief from it until the

FDA arrived. At that time, Scott was the top dog of the Maine egg industry and liaison with the FDA and state of Maine compliance. Tom O'Neill, Hugh Drummond, Andy Paven, and Ann Murphy handled the national government and public relations impeccably. We did not lose one business case and came out of the caustic situation maintaining our integrity and reputation with government officials, retail and food service customers, media, and consumers.

Now, back to the humane hit! We had to issue letters to our customers testifying to the conditions and policies of how we raise our chickens and handle our birds. Several supermarket executives ripped into me. Mark Lessard and Tim Jacques of Hannaford Brothers verbally hit me hard, but I knew I would make it out okay when Tim started with, "How come you didn't pick up the phone right away?" I told Tim he was not the first in line to rip my ass. I got a brief laugh, and then I took it on the chin.

Albertsons-Shaw's was pissed. They recalled the eggs and sent us a hefty bill. Jack Demoulas and Charlie Pappas of Market Basket were less caustic but certainly looking for a good deal for their belly-stuffer customer base, which we were happy to oblige. We had not heard from Walmart yet, but we knew it might be coming. So, I reached out to the buyer and notified them of an issue. I also called Eggland's Best Corporate QA Group and informed them. Eggland's Best was in complete damage control of the brand, and we knew that we were expendable if we did not survive from a press perspective despite the great partnership that we were involved with and built. My partners would throw us into the Atlantic Ocean if they felt it was in their best interest, notwithstanding the amount of innovation that we developed that was beneficial to their business.

The local and national media started calling us. I had only twenty minutes to think of something. I called Paul Shapiro from the HSUS in Washington and said, "How much time do you want?" I didn't even have to say to turn totally cage-free. Paul said seven years, and I said fifteen years. He said, "No f-cking way!" I said, "Let's compromise at ten years." It was done. The HSUS and our relationship saved our ass while laughing about it.

They were involved in the hit, but the HSUS's Josh Balk was with me in Maine lobbying for votes for the bill at the legislature. The executive director of the Brown Egg Council, Bill Bell, our legislative guru, found the person that hit us. I thought it was a real cheap shot and unnecessary, as we had the votes to pass the legislation in Maine. However, the animal rights interest groups had bigger ambitions, and we just rang a huge bell under duress. Wayne Pacelle issued a press statement praising our commitment to animal welfare with our ten-year commitment to transition to cage-free, while I called the media back and said that we were turning cage-free in ten years.

The US egg industry was pissed at first. I heard from Gene Gregory, president and CEO at the time of the United Egg Producers, after they had an urgent executive conference. He said, "What the hell did you do up there? This is definitely going to affect the entire industry. I am coming up, and we are going to have lunch to discuss this, David." I said, "Sure, Gene, love to see you." I did not say what I was thinking, which was that I was twenty minutes away from losing all of our business, and I had to go into complete damage control to save it. It wasn't like the association of allied industry was wrapping themselves around us to save our ass. That would not happen, and we did not get any love and kisses afterward.

Walmart was very pissed. They terminated our agreement, which was approximately a $700,000 annual contribution revenue hit that would have material adverse effects on our business. We needed to salvage what we could. I turned to Dave Gorman and Jorge Santos, who were board members with a strong record with Walmart. Dave was the former head of loss prevention at Walmart. I said, 'Ball's in your court, boys."

They immediately worked the system and had us write to people at higher levels. Soon, I got a call from the buyer who did not ask us whether we owned or leased the farm, which by now we didn't, as it was neighboring farmer Dorothy Egg Farm's lease. But, as politics go, owners John and Julia Lough were a Sam's supplier, and the boys and girls across the street from Walmart in Bentonville, Arkansas, were not bothering them about this.

We were able to get a meeting in Bentonville, and it was one of the most brutal interrogations that I have ever had. Kathi Brock and Tim Amlaw of American Humane were there with us, and we sincerely appreciated it. We were setting up humane training with our staff and closed-circuit television (CCTV), which was Gorman's suggestion. The American Humane Association booked the training with our company and Dorothy's company and funded the state inspectors so everyone was on the same page. State Vet Don Hoenig and Assistant State Vet Beth McEvoy were there too.

Tom Shea and Scott Burns ensured that we had proper CCTV installed in a test location first. I will cover this in greater detail later. We walked out of Walmart with the specialty business returning to us after the division executive met with the buyer and his boss. It was a no-win situation, as we went over the buyer's head, and he may have gotten disciplined for not checking first if we owned the facility before firing our ass. It was a shoot first and ask questions later environment down there. Walmart has stringent specifications for its customers, and they don't tolerate media that could hurt their business. They are straight and consistent about that.

Walmart committed to review the private label business and do a surprise inspection of our facilities in Maine. A few months later, it was cold as hell in winter, and I was at Sunday River in Maine for a day off of skiing with my family. I was sitting in a chair lift on the side of the mountain when I got the call. I immediately headed down the mountain, jumped into a car, and drove to Winthrop, about an hour away, where John Lough was already taking Walmart on a tour of certain facilities. Then, we took them to Leeds, Maine. After leaving Maine, they issued an inspection report that found some minor issues. Walmart never gave us the generic business back but let us keep the specialty business, including the Cage Free and Free Range eggs. We appreciated them for that business.

During this time of the initial press, I received a call from our Eggland's Best ownership cooperative of egg producers from the late Steve Michella, the SVP of Sales: "You survived! Cage-free in ten years. We thought you were dead to rights and absolutely done for, and you rose from the ashes."

Meanwhile, at the following industry meeting, Greg Hinton of Rose Acres was first to start laughing along with Jim Sumner of USAPEEC and Joanne Ivy, president of the American Egg Board. Doug and Kathy Wicker, who are great sponsors of Boys Farm, a local, sustainable charity worthy of support, also approached. Doug is a southern gentleman from Newbury, South Carolina, who sounds like the announcer for "Free Bird" at a Lynyrd Skynyrd concert. You know that guy that says, "Now what songgg is it you want to hear?" With a smile, he said, "Y'all been pretty busy in New England?"

"I had land that I hadn't built on yet in Jackson County, Georgia. David Lathem, my neighbor, said "Goodness David, they've been on you pretty good." Glenn Hickman from Arizona said "I get it. You were just trying to please everyone." Elliot Gibber of Deb El further egg processing said "Are you having fun yet?" Bob Pike from North Carolina said "Golly, they got you! Finally, Doug Richardson of Frost Accounting said "I figured you boys could use an audit!"

It was all cheerful smiles and chuckles about the statement and the survival except for one producer out west who took the party line of the UEP when he got "whacked." He was not happy with me at all, as I "didn't play by the national industry association rules and take one for the team." I worked with Al Pope, Gene Gregory, Chad Gregory, and Ken Klippen, when he was with UEP, to lobby on Capitol Hill supporting their legislative fund and lobby the White House, in addition to the work completed in Puerto Rico involving the lawsuit against the Puerto Rican government, noted in Chapter Three of this book, and at times support for Cuba.

In Cuba, we had some steady annual business. Still, we were looking to do a large deal with support from the UEP's US Egg Marketers affiliate to ship massive quantities at low prices, but that sale never materialized for Cuba. This situation caused the industry some lawsuits later for alleged collusion. Still, during these years, US Egg Marketers was a savior working with international businessman Jurgen Fuchs in cooperation with Charles and John Joyner of Dolphin Shipping. This international trading group acquired large quantities of eggs from US Egg Marketers. It sold them internationally for the industry during some unprofitable years. I never participated in any shipments with US Egg Marketers, and I was glad to be left out of the legal fun and games that ensued.

As president of the New England Brown Egg Council, I did lots of lobbying work throughout New England on behalf of the industry, so there were political considerations. The UEP benefited from the New England Brown Egg Council's diplomatic sustainable leadership support, given our strong relationships throughout New England with federal and state politicians. We had a longstanding relationship with our location in Georgia; we were a supportive addition to their extraordinary strength down there.

I was in a meeting with Gene Gregory, who was the president at the time. Gene did not mince words in describing the egg industry's displeasure with my going cage-free statement. "I told you that they [the HSUS] could not be trusted and that they would screw you and us," Gene said. It was groundbreaking and served as a bell ringer in the industry that would cause it to change from battery cages to either cage-free or enriched cages sooner than they wanted to. It was a big deal for egg producers, given that they needed to depreciate their housing systems over their life. A sooner date could cause producers a lot of disruption if the industry had the billions needed to make the change to totally cage-free systems. It's a big deal for egg producers given they typically need to fully depreciate their housing systems or finish their lease commitments before acquiring new equipment. There are no government programs handing producers in the aggregate billions of dollars to make these mandated changes to cage-free systems. Each farming producer has to finance it themselves. Think of the situation like mandating that you renovate your house and business operations without the money to pay for it. The HSUS was not going away. They could threaten the livelihood of any producer, distributor, and marketer with loss of business or failure from the negative press from a twenty-four-hour news cycle. The HSUS could also win in referendum states.

In 2011, UEP cut a deal for national legislation to eliminate battery cages and move to enriched colony "condo" cages as a compromise with the HSUS and seamlessly work to have a conversion date so producers would not have their replacement schedules disrupted with a convertible colony-caged system. The equipment manufacturers and installers worked hard to satisfy all agriculture with equipment updates such as QC Supply, of which I am now a limited partner and advisor working alongside Charlesbank Capital Partners, and Joe Fortin and Dave Newman's Northeast Agri Systems, along with various equipment companies that saw a newfound business with the equipment changes and worked hard to incubate and accelerate for the benefit of agriculture. Meanwhile, the National Pork Producers fought the colony cage deal. Why not, it's not their money. In my humble view, they had no business getting in the way of egg producers and costing them billions. They defended the slippery slope on Capitol Hill, and the bacon tripped up the eggs. The legislation died, and efforts ceased in 2013.

Without a deal with the industry, the situation spurred the HSUS back to the mandatory cage-free push nationally. The market opened to free-range birds, which gave them outdoor access. This change led to the next big growth area, which was a long-term success model. The HSUS took the statement that I made about a ten-year conversion under duress as a footprint and moved to accelerate it nationwide after the pork producers got in the way of a sound deal between the industry and the HSUS.

Close to every major grocery chain committed to change. Before that, Marcus Rust and Greg Hinton of Rose Acres Farms, one of the nation's highest-volume producers, committed to transition to cage-free to serve their customers' requirements. Other producers did as well. The chickens were let out of the barn as the race started to turn the US into a cage-free nation, which resulted in the socially progressive cage-free purchasers looking for something more in free-range and pasture-raised.

CHAPTER SEVEN

Civil Wars Break Out in Massachusetts at the Apex from Incubation to Acceleration of Cage Free Nation and Alternative Sustainable Protein

In the early part of the 2010 decade, not knowing that the dominoes were going to fall so fast, the HSUS tried to push their agenda in Massachusetts. Bill Bell, the executive director of the Brown Egg Council, was indispensable during all of these matters in getting the right people to do things the right way at the right time for the right reason in the political and legislative world. He introduced me to one of the lead Massachusetts farming executives. I met with the executive about cutting a "grandfather deal" like what was negotiated in Maine. The discussion went something like this at the home of the late Henry Gillette, a former state representative and lobbyist. From what I recall, he said words to the effect of, "You're caving to the enemy, Radlo, and it is wrong that any industry, anyone, or any farmer would do that. You should be ashamed of yourself."

In this situation, I represented the New England Brown Egg Council producers and distributors as president and had the backing of the UEP. I interpreted his statements as a personal attack. I responded in kind: "You have absolutely no f-cking skin in the game. You don't have your farms and supply hit and have your customers threatened or lost, because you get paid to get into fights and not resolve them and play slippery slope bullsh-t willing to be the sacrificial lamb in a national chess match and beat your f-cking chest and say the HSUS is the enemy while you knowingly want to take on and lose a referendum unless Massachusetts does better than California, where the industry got crushed in a similar ballot initiative."

From what I recall, he responded by saying "F-ck you." I responded with my sincerest best wishes and warmest regards! Henry and Bill quickly got in the middle as it was getting quite heated, and we were toe-to-toe. So much for a friendly discussion to settle issues. Bill and Henry made a noble effort to get us together to resolve the matter, but it looks like it was an NFW (no f-cking way) deal.

I had a good friend and neighbor from Lexington, MA, named Don Wilson. Unfortunately, he recently passed away, but he and his great family, including his brother Al and the next generation led by Scott, have been a symbol of sustainable leadership and all things people, process, and strategy. They grew tremendous farm-side fruits, vegetables, meats, and specialty items along with a wholesale business for generations with Wilson Farm. www.wilsonfarm.com.

They transitioned to cage-free and took charge from then on in dealing with the said executive from that point further. In Chapter Five of *Principles of Cartel Disruption*, I discuss the benefits of using the Innermetrix Behavioral Analysis. This analysis assists organizations in understanding and utilizing people resources. The assessment shows I have zero empathy during stressful situations, and this situation was no exception.

Novelist V. S. Naipaul, in *A Bend in the River*, wrote, "When all endeavor is futile, what use, what consequence is one's action?" Fighting the HSUS is futile, especially in a referendum state where they would raise the money, put a cage-free initiative on the ballot, and win. Therefore, it is counterproductive to fight them. Also, an undercover investigative video could ruin your business, whether it was a setup or not.

Below is with Maine State Vet Don Hoenig and Assistant State Vet Beth McEvoy; Kathi Brock and Tim Amlaw of American Humane; and Scott Burns and John Stevens, who drove food safety and animal welfare along with team members. The training was tied in with the states of Maine and Massachusetts. It was another bell ringer and a proud day of American Humane animal welfare training with Maine and Massachusetts farmers of the New England Brown Egg Council. It delighted us to have this farmer-state-animal welfare partnership that has accelerated nationally since this inaugural incubation event.

AMERICAN HUMANE CERTIFIED
HISTORIC FIRST ANIMAL WELFARE
TRAINING CLASS
10-26-09

First Row: **Norma Worley**, Director, Animal Welfare Programs, State of Maine; **Sue Metzger**, District Humane Agent; **Don Hoenig**, VMD, State Veterinarian, State of Maine; **Wendy Weirich**, DVM, American Humane Instructor; **David Radlo**, CEO, Radlo Foods; **Kathi Brock**, Marketing Director American Humane Certified; **Jennifer Howlett**, Humane Agent, State of Maine; **Beth McEvoy**, DVM Asst. State Veterinarian, State of Maine

Second Row: **Howard Edgecomb**, Radlo Foods; **Matt Jones**, American Humane Instructor; **Rollin Straton**, Radlo Foods; **Nick Labrie**, Radlo Foods; **Everett Weaver**, Radlo Foods; **Bill Morrison**, Poultry Specialist, Maine Dept. of Agriculture; **Cliff Smith**, Barn Manager, Radlo Foods; **Scott Burns**, Animal Welfare and Food Safety Director, Radlo Foods; **John Stevens**, Manager, Radlo Foods; **Chrissy Perry**, District Humane Agent; **Aseem Chandawarkar**, American Humane Certified; **Tim Amlaw**, Director, American Humane Certified

Not Pictured: **Don Wilson**, Owner, Wilson Farms, Lexington, Mass.; **Cindy Kilgore**, Livestock Specialist, Maine Dept. of Agriculture; **Bill Bell**, New England Brown Egg Council

PHOTO 7.A.
American Humane Training in New England

Massachusetts "Egg-mageddon": Background to a Crisis and Strange Bedfellows

There were agriculture association leaders nationally and in Massachusetts that espoused fighting everything. It's called the "slippery slope" doctrine of lobbying. They will fight everything to cause the other side to expend resources, and therefore incremental change will take longer. The fear is that once they deal with one issue, they will take up another issue that may hurt them a lot. In this situation, the slippery slope folks effectively threw the egg industry under the bus as the Massachusetts Farm Bureau (MFB) and the National Pork Producers won the agriculture fight. Massachusetts didn't make a deal similar to the one made in Maine with the HSUS. Allied agriculture or not, they failed to reach an agreement with the HSUS and the Massachusetts Society for the Prevention of Cruelty to Animals (MSPCA) to settle. The two allied animal rights groups carried out their threat and brought the matter by initiative petition.

When the matter came to a referendum, the voters in Massachusetts voted in favor of all products sold in Massachusetts being produced cage-free. Question three on the ballot in 2016 had a definite date for integration that ended up being January 1, 2022. The veal farmers are already in conversion. The pork guys missed their opportunity to push out the effective compliance date and have the agreement only apply to production and not sales, where 99% of the egg and pork production comes from out of state! It is exceedingly costly for the industry, in the hundreds of millions of dollars, for unnecessary new farm equipment. This situation wouldn't have happened if a deal was reached.

Congratulations. Nice job, MFB! What could you possibly be thinking? The slippery slope rationale should not allow the opposition to walk across the goal line to the end zone. Cutting a deal would effectively not place a ban on 99% of the product being sold into the state and preserve less than 1% produced in the state by grandfathering. Given that the MFB leadership did not have skin in the game, the egg farmers were the ones footing the bill from transitioning to cage-free with no support or assistance from federal or state governments. The MFB argued by championing a referendum fight for a more rapid transition that would cost producers that ship into the state their portion of the $7.8–$9.5 billion in incremental cage-free equipment costs and knowingly increase the price of a needed staple of the poor.[8] Some groups can't see the forest because the "slippery slope" trees are in the way.

Believe it or not, the law passed by initiative petition by a vast margin, and Massachusetts will indeed plan on banning all non-cage-free eggs on January 1, 2022. The United Egg Producers and the New England Brown Egg Council have been working since 2019 to make technical changes to the law to mirror positive changes in technology for multi-tiered housing at 1.0 square foot per hen, which is the United States industry standard for cage-free. The current law passed by the initiative petition was 1.5 square feet on the floor, which is different from the current national standard of 1.0 square foot of space in multi-tiered housing.

Other items are in the works, such as a scratch area and perch area in cooperation with the HSUS and MSPCA so that there will not be shortages during this period. If there is a shortage of eggs during this transition or perhaps the increased prices for eggs may cause consumers to travel to neighboring states to shop, it will be incredibly challenging for low-income consumers and people who can't travel to get eggs, a staple in many homes.

Lobbyist Richard Tisei and Jim Isenberg of Preti Strategies (Richard is a former legislator I worked with during the H. W. campaign of 1988), took over after lobbyist Henry Gillette passed away. According to industry sources, Bill Cass of the Suffolk Group joined to represent the allied egg industry with the local Massachusetts Grocers Association. In addition, these technical proposed amendments have the support of the initiative petition sponsors, the HSUS, and the MSPCA.

According to industry sources, former Congressman Chester Atkins represents the other side. The Humane Farming Association (HFA), a California-based animal rights group, filed a lawsuit against the Massachusetts Attorney General's Office to enforce the 1.5 square feet of space passed by initiative petition. Making strange bedfellows, so to speak, the MFB has been paradoxically supportive of the legislative initiatives of the HFA in this regard for the rationale described below.

The UEP and the New England Brown Egg Council made efforts to bring the MFB on board. Without an agricultural interest consensus, politicians generally sideline bills such as the one for more implementation time or technical changes in the law before it goes into effect. In Massachusetts, the bill ended up in "study," similar to the federal legislation mandating "enriched cages" or group housing that was sidelined because the pork industry lobbied against the egg equipment change, which hence has caused a more costly alternative with mandatory cage-free systems.

According to the attached memorandum, Brad Mitchell, an MFB executive, may have gotten into a disagreement via phone with UEP President and CEO Chad Gregory. Mitchell and the MFB are in the mode of payback. Mitchell stated, "We don't support changing what we consider a bad law before it has had a chance to exhibit itself as such," after being warned by the MFB that it would "raise the cost of food." His statement was a response to the proposed technical changes in the law that would avert a potential crisis as the MFB was on the losing side of the referendum.

As noted, the net effect of this will cause on and after January 1, 2022, the residents of the state of Massachusetts to cross state lines to Nashua and Seabrook, NH; Pawtucket, RI; Hartford, CT; the Albany area in NY; and Brattleboro, VT, to get eggs in states that don't have this law. In addition, local Massachusetts retailers will have fewer sales on all of their breadbaskets after enactment due to likely shortages of eggs. Once consumers change where they shop, Massachusetts retailers may see a long-term loss of business.

It's coming down to the wire, and the industry has been working tirelessly in meetings with the Governor's Office, the speaker of the House, and the president of the Senate, in addition to chairs and members of key committees, with less than a few months before implementation into law. Suppliers need to plan in advance to meet the demand, and key farmers and distributors like Hillandale Farms of Connecticut have invested $85M in new cage-free aviary systems.[9] There is plenty on the governor's and legislature's plate with Covid-19 and budgetary issues. There is only so much time in the day.

In 2021, the matter turned public as the *Boston Globe* questioned whether Massachusetts consumers should "brace for Egg-mageddon. There is no way to know for sure. The pandemic sure taught us we shouldn't take household staples for granted. It's more of a challenge to stock up on eggs than toilet paper."[10] The Farm Bureau and HFA may be strange bedfellows but are on the same side of this issue.

The Bethel family of Hillandale Farms that supply most of Massachusetts with eggs have invested in the national standard for cage-free and they certainly attempt to do all that they can to meet customer requirements. But the pace of henhouse construction slowed due to social distancing requirements and outbreaks of Covid-19. The point of no return has already passed, as the egg industry has not budged off of the 1.0 national cage-free standard and is in a position to ship eggs to other states instead starting in January of 2022.

The Massachusetts Senate passed the measure in June of 2021 to avert the crisis, and facing a food supply crisis, the House passed the legislation by the margin of 156-1 on October 6, 2021. The bill included a measure to allow pork producers to have another year to phase in. and the bill is headed to conference with the Senate to work-out their differences and to Governor Baker for signature. Regardless of whether or not the law is changed to stop "Eggmageddon," the HFA has stated that they intend to force another ballot initiative with the original language. According to Jasper Goodman of the *Boston Globe*, on June 25, 2021, Brad Mitchell of the Massachusetts Farm Bureau aligned with the HFA. Mitchell stated, "This is what a few special interests have temporarily agreed on at this spot in time." Bill Bell, executive director of the New England Brown Egg Council, said, "I am glad this passed. The Connecticut Farm Bureau issued a statement in support of this bill, and I really want to continue to stick this up Brad Mitchell's ass." Regardless, due to the HFA threats for another referendum, the matter in Massachusetts will continue for years to come.

Please see attached *Exhibit 7.1. "Chad and Brad Fight"**

From: Chad Gregory [mailto:~~~~~~~~~~~~~~~]
Sent: Friday, November 01, 2019 3:06 PM
To: brad~~~~~~~; mark~~~~~~~; doug~~~~~~
Cc: Bill Bell; Mike Sencer; Bob Beauregard
Subject: Shocked!

Brad,

I am shocked at the hostile nature you approached our conversation just now. I am shocked you took an immediate "defensive" position and came out swinging with innuendoes and hateful accusations. You repeatedly said I was "bullshitting" you and insinuating I was lying to you. None of this was remotely close to the truth...despite what you believe or have been led to believe.

It has been 2-3 years since you and I spoke last and I wanted to call to share our (UEP) position directly (as opposed to through Bill Bell or rumors) on the Mass. egg legislation and also get your opinion/position. But from the very beginning you were HOT - angry, borderline screaming into the phone and rude. I couldn't even get two words in without being interrupted by you with your preconceived opinions about me, my beliefs and this legislation. Of which you have no clue about because you weren't listening and you apparently don't have an open mind – you were too busy screaming.

What happened to the day when two professionals, both representing farmers, could have a civil conversation and at the end still agree to disagree but at least both sides got to share their view? This is precisely what is wrong with this country.

The worst part of our conversation (not really a conversation when you spent the entire time yelling at me) is when at the end I asked you – a Farm Bureau employee – "Brad are you not in favor of trying to reverse of bad law that uneducated voters passed to something that is better for farmers or citizens" and you said "NO". That is shocking that a farm bureau employee would prefer really bad laws to go into effect vs. trying to reverse, educate or fix those bad laws.

Unfortunately, we will be on opposite sides on this one. I am VERY concerned about the 7 million people – your neighbors, friends, family and coworkers – in Mass having choices taken away from them AND paying $8-$10 per dozen of eggs in 2022 because there is an extreme shortage. I am trying to get a law passed that keeps food affordable. Stunning to me that you – a farm bureau employee - are opposed to trying to keep food affordable in your state. You want the opposite – you apparently want food to be extremely expensive.

I completely understand that professionals can have varying opinions on something and remain civil. Wish you would have approached my call that way. If you would have, at the end of the call I would have completely respected you and your side/position. Unfortunately because of your anger and unprofessionalism, I cannot and will not respect you or your side.

Chad Gregory
President and CEO
United Egg Producers

*Memorandums from Chad Gregory of the United Egg Producers to Brad Mitchell of the Massachusetts Farm Bureau and Brad Mitchell to Chad Gregory. (I obtained these documents from an industry source relative to a long inter-industry fight that led up to the situation.)

From: Brad Mitchell [ma~~ilto:~~ ~~~~]
Sent: Friday, November 01, 2019 6:50 PM
To: Chad Gregory
Cc: mark~~~~; doug~~~~; Bill Bell; Mike Sencer; Bob Beauregard
Subject: Re: Shocked!

Chad,

I was equally shocked by the manner in which you approached this. I've had numerous conversations with folks who are your side of this legislation (retailers, food association, etc) and they have been civil with each of us understanding the perspective of the other in representing the interests of our constituents.

None, have taken the approach you did with me which was to make statements such as you did in this email such as ".you - a farm bureau employee are opposed to trying to keep food affordable in yourstate." !Do you consider this to be professional behavior? Nor did I say I was ""... trying to reverse of bad law that uneducated voters passed to something that is better for farmers or citizens". I would suggest that it is your penchant for hyperbole and leading statements such as this that made our cal go so badly.

And let's be honest. You are far less interested in keeping food affordable for MA citizens than ensuring the market her is open to your members. As I said, I respect that - it's your job. I also have a job which is to represent the wishes of my constituents which in this instance conflict with those of yours.

As I explained, before I was forced to wish you a good weekend and hang up on you ranting:

1. This is not my position. It is that of our members.

2. Farm Bureau is not opposed to affordable food or fixing bad laws. However, The standards about to go into place were voted in by a vast majority of voters. While MA Farm Bureau oppose Q3- a) we do respect the will of the voters;2) they were warned (mostly by MA Farm Bureau) that this would raise the cost of food. What I said was that we don't support changing what we consider a bad law before it has had a chance to to exhibit itself as such - especially when voted in specifically by the citizens.

Again, have a good weekend. Again, if we speak again I hope our interaction goes better.

Brad

[Quoted text hidden]

National Animal Rights Victory and Beyond

In 2016, Wayne Pacelle of the HSUS achieved a historic victory that I had predicted ten years earlier. When Walmart made a statement and pledged to go cage-free following other supermarkets, the battle was nearly over. Other animal agriculture farmer industries were playing ball with the HSUS, except for pork and organizations like the MFB. Our humane Free Roaming milk pushed the dairy industry into better conditions along with certain Prince of Darkness-inspired videos. The HSUS had victories in veal crates too. The agriculture industry was turning, in the eyes of the humane society, more humane.

Pacelle and the HSUS wrote to me in 2016 and noted the same: "Roughly ten years ago, you had the courage to meet with me when few egg producers would do the same. You predicted that the future would be cage-free and you believed the egg industry should work with us to achieve this inevitable future. Shortly after Walmart announced its switching to 100% cage-free eggs and virtually every other major food company has done the same, I write to say you had tremendous foresight. I appreciate the open dialogue we've had over the years and you being a reasonable, thoughtful voice throughout."

Gene Gregory's son Chad is a great guy too, but he's more of a politician. He's careful with his words, but I give him credit on the exchange with Mitchell for sticking up for what is right not only in the industry but also for the poor and all retail consumers. I love having him aboard when he's available for international trade meetings with USAPEEC'S Jim Sumner.

Apex Point from Industry Incubation to Acceleration of Cage-free

In 2016 at the apex point from incubation to acceleration, the public cage-free commitments of retail and food service customers in the egg industry was an additional $190M or 66% of the current flock. Since Walmart has made a cage-free announcement, and several states have either voted by initiative petition or implemented laws to turn cage-free by 2025, the country is transitioning to be a cage-free nation from free-range to pasture-raised.

According to USDA agricultural analytics, cage-free shell production accounted for 9.9% of current table egg layers (30 million hens). According to the UEP, there will be 190.41 million more cage-free layers or over 51 billion more cage-free eggs, representing 66% of the flock. However, this number is understated as it does not take into account organic egg growth and the effects of mandatory legislation, such as in Massachusetts and several other states.

Based on these numbers and the assumption that the replacement cost per bird is $40–$50, the projected equipment growth would be $7.62B–$9.52B required to supply and finance current customer commitments to go cage-free, notwithstanding the additional growth stated above and any new obligations. The costs don't include the parts that will follow the new equipment.

In 2021, the commitment to go cage-free is one thing, but financing the multi-billions it will take to turn to a cage-free nation is another issue. Egg farmers with a fifteen-to-twenty-year depreciation level on their equipment may get caught in the middle without a bank willing to finance the change. This situation will cause more consolidation of the industry as larger firms with the financing—or those that are so big that banks can't let them go under during bad markets—acquire the smaller ones that do not have the resources during this transition.

Current and Future Attractions: What Does David See in His Crystal Ball?

Better Meat CEO Paul Shapiro tweeted on July 22, 2021, "I was right all along," about projections of future acceptance of humane products such as cage-free, free-range, pasture-raised, and alternative protein products. In the future, I foresee the vegan nation synergistically partnering with environmental sustainability to drive the growth of non-animal-based options at double-digit growth while taxing animal agriculture to level the playing field. This innovation will accelerate their growth even further. You can now get some fantastic-tasting, plant-based meat in the supermarket or at your favorite burger joint, such as Dan Brown's Beyond Meat. Arturo Elizondo and John Farmer of Clara Foods and Josh Balk's side gig with Josh Tetrick are whipping up creations from Eat Just and are embarking on non-animal eggs.

From the Tufts Friedman School of Nutrition Entrepreneurship Advisory Board, my big-funded corporate colleagues and entrepreneurs alike are in high gear as well, backed by Angel and Venture Capital. Such great interest and passion come from Uma Valeti, the CEO of Memphis Meats; Jimena Florez of Chaak; and Kevin Boylan of the Veggie Grill, PowerPlant Ventures, and many more. The money behind the vision and partnership is supported by Bob Stringer of Crimson Seed Capital, Lauren Abda of Branch Foods, Peter Boyce of General Catalyst, Jim Miller of MassChallenge, and Shawn Broderick's Food-X, as well as funders folks like UNFI's Matt Whitney, with health-related and sustainable big interest from Jason Camm, the chief medical officer for Peter Thiel. Senior advisors like Bill Layden, Carlos Barroso, Heather Terry, Ashley Koff, and Irwin Heller are always there to lend a helping hand. They provide great value propositions, money, and tremendous advice to incubate and accelerate per *Principles* of Cartel Disruption: "Accelerate and Maximize Performance."

Branching into a safer, new, and better world, are former Bluebird CEO Dr. Alfred Slanetz, now of Geneius Biotechnology, with groundbreaking "T-cell immunotherapy for successful treatment of cancer patients," according to Crunchbase, and Dr. Siyaram Pandey of the University of Windsor (Canada), who uses natural compounds and PTS technology to treat Parkinson's, Alzheimer's, and other ailments.

Meanwhile, Better Meat CEO Paul Shapiro has disrupted industry partners Perdue and others with the "clean meat revolution," as displayed in his book *Clean Meat: How Growing Meat without Animals Will Revolutionize Dinner and the World*. How does it taste? Commercially, that issue is being addressed with impressive results. In June of 2021, Shapiro unveiled a newly created fermentation facility in West Sacramento, California, that turns out minimally processed whole food mycoprotein called Rhiza that is "cheaper than beef . . . [has] more protein than eggs . . . more fiber than oats . . . [is] non-GMO . . . with the goal to reduce the human footprint on the planet."[11] His wife, Toni Okamoto, has released *The Friendly Vegan Cookbook* and two others. Social progressives need to pay their bills too. If they follow Chapters One through Eleven in *Principles of Cartel Disruption* and understand the cartel rules from this book, they will easily leapfrog the "Valley of Death" that Bill Gates refers to in his new book, *How to Avoid a Climate Disaster: The Solutions We Have and the Breakthroughs We Need.*[12]

Social progression causes ever-changing value propositions that drive innovation and acceleration. Motivated vegans, led by Prince of Darkness Paul, Josh, and excited young entrepreneurs like Arturo and John, are masters of this new food protein category. As noted in *Principles of Cartel Disruption*, plant-based meat data showed a projected Year Over Year Category Growth projected at 31% in the US and 20% in Europe through 2025. Caroline Bushnell of the Good Food Institute stated at the USAPEEC meeting on June 24, 2021, that "plant-raised, fermentation, and cultivated segments are positioned for strong growth. Plant-based meats are projected based upon BCG and BLUE Horizon at 10–11% by 2035, while Cargill is projecting that within three to four years they will be perhaps 10% of the market."

Now they are positioning to accelerate further by synergistically partnering for environmental sustainability and reducing the carbon footprint. The progressives are also taking advantage of taste improvements, driving out costs with scale, Bushnell says, on cultivated meats with 10X–100X cost reductions, while taking advantage of the higher prices of humane animal agriculture food.

The acceleration trumpets of vegans have sounded to lower to zero-carbon-equivalent-emission products using clean plant and lab-based options. Bill Gates is a champion for them. Every angle is covered, while green investors like Bill Gates are left cheering. Zero-carbon equivalent emissions or bust, Bill! We will eat our way out of a climate change disaster! The Prince of Darkness and Gates's "Kool-Aid" doesn't taste that bad now and is improving.

As Gates proposes to level the playing field:

We can reduce Green Premiums by making carbon-free things cheaper, by making carbon-emitting things more expensive, or by doing some of both by progressively increasing the price of carbon to reflect its true cost; governments can nudge producers and consumers toward more efficient decisions and encourage innovation that reduces the Green Premium.[13]

The pain or pleasure of social progressive gravity is coming sooner than you think and you will need every dime and take smart action to accelerate your growth performance whether you are an opportunistic innovating Cartel Disruptor, Sustainable Leader, or Dominant Market or Cartel Leader.

Your Turn for Action to Improve Yourself and Your Chance to Vote:

Take the free Radlo Achievement Index found on DavidRadlo.com. Click on the assessment tab. When you take the assessment, you will receive immediate feedback. You are also welcome to vote for or leave your favorite name for the Carbon Equivalent Tax such as:

1. *VARCEE (Value Added Reduction in Carbon Equivalent Emissions)*
2. *GWI (Global Warming Investment)*
3. *CCIT (Climate Change Investment Tax)*
4. *GatesCare*
5. *GreenCare*
6. *GMSF (Green Marketing Services Fee)*
7. *GCET (Green Carbon Equivalent Tax or the Gates Carbon Equivalent Tax)*
8. *CET (Carbon Equivalent Tax)*
9. *WWCET (World-Wide Carbon Equivalent Tax)*
10. *Your Name*

Bill Gates articulated the big problem, and we have big taxes coming our way with some friendly regulations and mandates. We need the correct value proposition name, as Chapter One of *Principles of Cartel Disruption* notes, to inspire the world to pay for global warming or climate change. Rest assured, governments may work together and find numerous ways to scale, tax, and enforce the tax, so they can test market, incubate, accelerate, and create trillions in new taxable revenue to offset climate change.

Would you characterize that as a massive cartel action to save the planet from climate change? Or would you describe it as worldwide Socialism driving costs to operate and increased regulations? As Fidel Castro said, "*Socialismo o muerte, decide!*" (Socialism or death, you decide!). Ironically, Castro was very concerned with policies that drastically increase sustainable feed prices that have a detrimental worldwide effect on the poor, such as with biofuels. I spent hours with him and his vice president, Carlos Lage, discussing the subject.

I will have to ponder that as I sit here sleeping forty yards from the water at Point Del Sol on Cape Cod. My mind says, "Don't bet against Bill Gates backing vegan and environmental-social progressive action."

CHAPTER EIGHT

The Biggest Strategic Planning and Execution Mistake in Consumer Food and Agriculture Product Marketing History

Specialty Egg Powerhouse Fights Socially Progressive Gravity

We had a lot to be thankful for as Radlo Foods prepared to exit a portion of the egg and related food business. With the help of our outstanding board, as noted in Chapter Ten of *Principles of Cartel Disruption*, what started to be roughly $10M in sales manifested into close to $102M in the business of consolidated commodity and specialty products. In addition, the brands Born Free and Eggland's Best sustained double-digit growth.

The following excellent group of specialists made it happen:

Sales: Patrick Magagnos, Jim LeRoy, Rafi Velez, Nicky McKinney, the late Jim Corbin, Jim Ryan, Jim Harmon, C. A. Dapolite, Bruce McKee, Paul Bologna, Tom Bowden, Eric Puhacz, and Johnny Harris

Marketing and Strategic Planning: Mark Shuster (Outside BOD-Execution), Tony DeLio (Outside BOD-Strategic Partnerships & Alliances), Jorge Santos (Outside BOD-Ventures and Strategic Planning), Dan Rogers (Strategic Planning and Development-BOD), Bob Goehrke (Outside BOD-30,000 feet), Lisa Fraser (BOD), and Marketing QB Joan Leroy, assisted by Laura Cope and Lenore Romer.

Operational Execution: Tom Shea (SVP), Scott Burns (chief I.T. and Food Safety officer), John Stevens, Roe Cote, the late Dave Sanborn, Gay Smith, and the late John Ricca.

Finance, Administration, and Growth Platforms: Paul Gisbourne (CFO and BOD), Steph Norton (SVP-Admin and BOD), Dave Gorman (Outside BOD), John Brzezenski (Outside BOD), Valerie Vastis, and Sandy Porter, along with Maria Saxe, Karen Fisher, and Mirna Erazo.

PR, Government, and Political Advisory: Tom O'Neill, Hugh Drummond, Ann Murphy, and Andy Paven in New England and Phil Olsson, David Durkin, Gus Schumacher (Outside BOD), and Christine Bushway (Outside BOD) in Washington, DC.

Real Estate and Deal Advisory: John Hampton (BOD) and Judge Larry Warhall (retired).

As noted in *Principles of Cartel Disruption*, Chapter Ten, on selecting a talented board to maximize results, we ingrained in our board (BOD) assistance with functional areas. We gave it roll-up-your-sleeves projects in addition to board duties and committees to maximize results. Many of our partners and the greater sustainable community coast to coast benefited on a multiple of X basis to what we created and accelerated to do our part to sustainably transform for a Safer, New, and Better World.

The Born Free brand went from zero to almost $18.5M according to Nielsen syndicated data, listed in exhibit 7.A. below. It grew rapidly for fifty-two weeks, ending September 2012 when the deal was signed. The growth didn't include Walmart sales nationally or hard-boiled eggs, liquid eggs, or dairy sales.

Brand growth was at 16.8% in sales revenue, 16.6% in units. It was trending upward with 25.2% in revenue growth and 26.9% unit growth for the last twenty-four weeks. The dairy sales held their own and expanded. There was also an opportunity for growth. The overall brand was second in the Boston ADI market with solid penetration in New York and the Carolinas. There was national acceptance with Free Range and Free Range Organic. Business growth and same-store sales were robust. We had ourselves a socially progressive Certified Humane hit on our hands headed for great national success as I got up in the morning thinking how to create the next multi-billion-dollar industry.

For comparison purposes, when we exited the Eggland's Best Partnership, Nielsen syndicated data showed $517M in revenue growing at 16.5% and 9.6% in units for fifty-two weeks for the brand non-Walmart. For twenty-four weeks, it showed 14.9% in sales revenue and 8% in unit revenue.

However, it was a humbling start. In the Boston ADI market, after some failures in test markets over a few years, we implemented plastic dozen Cage Free, plastic Cage Free Organic six-packs after the paper six-packs failed, and, eventually, China-white cartons for regular Eggland's Best six-packs. In addition, we used Styrofoam for the Large and X-Large eggs and eighteen-pack "bonus 6 eggs free" at times. We replicated the successful packaging and marketing mix nationally and with accelerated blockbuster success! As part of investing considerably with finance, time, and talents on this footprint launch, Radlo Foods secured the grandfather rights to Born Free and private label lines from my partners, the producer group Eggland's Best.

About the same time as my exit, some owner/franchisees followed my lead and reached a similar conclusion that the timing was right to exit. I am proud to be a part of this double-digit growth success story for multiple years. We turned a small niche of a large category into its own big category by itself. We also incubated and accelerated specialty hard-boiled lines and other products commonly referred to as the "cherry, hot fudge, and whipped cream" products to complement shell egg "ice cream."

We had a dedication to giving back to causes like the Susan G. Komen Breast Cancer Foundation (https://www.komen.org). As part of a national effort with many of my producing partners affiliated with Eggland's Best, the UEP, the Brown Egg Council, and the American Egg Board, Radlo Foods gave millions of eggs as donations to local food banks, including the Greater Boston Foodbank (https://www.gbfb.org), Providence Foodbank (https://rifoodbank.org), Manchester Food Bank, (https://nhfoodbank.org/manchester/), and Good Shepherd Food Bank in Maine, (https://www.gsfb.org). As stated in Chapter Eleven of *Principles of Cartel Disruption*, giving back with your time, talents, money, goods, and services is the noble and just thing to do. The producing partners continue to do more as the local communities require.

In *Principles of Cartel Disruption* Chapter Nine, "Developing Exit Strategies," I cover reasons why a business owner would consider exiting their business. Based on public information, in the case of Radlo Foods, the reason that we can publicly share is that the skus had reached a point of saturation. Some targeted media advertising was aimed at older consumer groups, so there were potential losses due to consumers' natural causes of death. The loss of this market would affect growth with our traditional products. We believed that it was getting close to the highest value to sell.

We sold to an honorable, strategic partner, Land O'Lakes, and their subsidiary Moark, to outstanding executives Craig Willardson and Alan Dicks, under Chris Polinski and Dan Knutson, with special assistance from Ric Sundal. So today, Land O'Lakes is out of the egg production business, and my partnership and franchise areas were sold or assigned to my good friends and former partners Gary Bethel of Hillandale Farms and Dolph Baker of Cal-Maine Foods.

However, as part of renewal negotiations for their subsidiary Moark's franchise rights before their divestiture of the egg production business, Land O'Lakes licensed their egg brand rights to Eggland's Best's producer partnership. According to publicly released information, they became a 50% financial partner of Eggland's Best LLC, paying a reported $126M mid-year 2012. Beth Ford, an outstanding executive and industry leader, is at the helm now as CEO of Land O'Lakes, and I can't say enough about the company and its impeccable reputation both in the industry and to the consumer.

Around this time, Land O'Lakes felt it best that we grow the Born Free and Certified Humane Free Range niche and come back to sell it to them after we took it to the next level. Land O'Lakes was direct. They felt the brand and Certified Humane Free Range niche was not a threat to anyone and was the size of "a pimple on a horse's ass," but they said it was impressive that we had 30% of the brand size of the Land O'Lakes brand overall. It was growing faster, and we were spending 50–70% less than they were on advertising and promotions. Our pricing with Free Range was comparatively much higher than their Cage Free and Cage Free Organic.

Our board and the Land O'Lakes management spent quite a bit of time on strategic planning. I discuss strategic planning in-depth in Chapter Four of *Principles of Cartel Disruption*. Proper planning was leading to great prospects for the future of the business. We believed the future growth was in Certified Humane Free Range, Organic, and Pasture Raised based on the numbers. As the generic eggs transitioned to Cage Free, the progressive social customers wanted something better and higher priced. We were also the first commercial Certified Humane Free Range and Free Roaming dairy. We were the only game in town with such offerings, and the growth was strong — headed for a rocket ship ride.

We signed an agreement with the Land O'Lakes subsidiary to sell them Eggland's Best ownership and franchise rights, with a grandfather exemption to allow us to stay in business and market Born Free and Certified Humane Free Range. We sold domestically throughout the United States and kept our export business running. We were selling domestically and internationally to Canada, Puerto Rico, Cuba, other parts of Bermuda and the Caribbean, the Middle East, Hong Kong, and Europe.

Eggland's Best management, backed by the producer board operating the company, did not want to focus on the growth of Free Range, Free Range Organic, and the Free Range-Pasture Raised Certified Humane niche; they had no interest in acquiring Born Free. Still, with the sale of our Eggland's Best franchise and ownership rights, the Eggland's Best management, under the producer board's control and operation, reviewed the sale. To get a deal done, we agreed to exit the business entirely. It was a unique set of circumstances heading into an across-the-board owner-franchise agreement negotiation.

This period was a draining emotional roller coaster. At the same time, I had family members that were ill and one that passed away. After taking the time to reflect and pray about what was best for the family, I made the extremely difficult decision to quickly sell the Born Free and Free Range Certified Humane product line, along with our export business, to an investment company affiliated with our investment banker. I signed a multiyear noncompete and exited the business entirely. There were other circumstances involved that I will leave on the card table of the smoke-filled room, perhaps for another book. Or, if you join me at my favorite restaurant in Florida, Jacques and Tracy Klempf's Cowford Chophouse in Jacksonville, I may share.

In Chapter Four of *Principles of Cartel Disruption*, I discuss strategic planning trap errors. New Eggland's Best fell victim to several of them:

1. They failed to recognize and understand events and changing conditions in the competitive environment.

2. They based their strategies on a flawed set of assumptions.

3. They could not provide the leadership essential to successfully implementing strategic change through socially progressive gravity fighting.

The numbers speak for themselves. These errors continue to cost New Eggland's Best, its financial owners, and its producers billions of dollars in revenue and business value. Once we exited without their strong innovative disrupting force as part of the partnership, they didn't focus on customer results in the progressive sector of Free Range, Free Range Organic, and Free Range-Pasture Raised Certified Humane until they realized that they were running far behind and had to get into the game.

In addition, please review the Good, Better, and Best Grid from *Principles of Cartel Disruption*, Chapter One, "Understand Your Opportunity and Create a Winning Value Proposition," for context.

Exhibit 8.A. GOOD, BETTER BEST DIAGRAM
(Chart 1.3 of the Principles of Cartel Disruption).

Features

GOOD	BETTER	BEST
Vegetarian Fed	Omega	Eggland's Best Taste and Nutrition
Cage Free	Free Range	Pasture Raised | Organic

Packaging

GOOD	BETTER	BEST
Foam	Overlay	Plastic

Sizes

GOOD	BETTER	BEST
Small/Medium	Large/X-Large	Jumbo

Egg Color

GOOD	BETTER	BEST
White	Blue-Green	Brown

Amount

GOOD	BETTER	BEST
18 Pack or Larger	Dozen	6 Pack

The investment company we sold to did not adequately plan and finance the growth of Born Free and Commercial Certified Humane Free Range. As a result, the double-digit growth of the $20M brand came off the shelf along with the dairy and egg product items during the high season about a year later. You can find these strategic planning and new venture financing errors in Chapters Four and Eight of *Principles of Cartel Disruption*, where I discuss how to accelerate and maximize performance.

Meanwhile, my "Live Free or Die" neighbor in New Hampshire, Jesse Laflamme of Pete and Gerry's, capitalized on the successful brand Born Free and Free Range being taken off the shelf. He eventually hired my former employees Jim LeRoy, Eric Puhacz, and Johnny Harris to help accelerate growth and restage their Pete and Gerry's Organic and Nellie's Nest to Certified Humane Free Range instead of Cage Free. National explosive growth became a reality from these strategic moves.

The New Eggland's Best marketing management and producers sat on the sidelines watching this happen. They could've been the lead brand organically with Born Free with hundreds of millions of units and revenue annually and billions of Certified Humane Free Range product business value in branded and private label by supporting successful innovation. Further, sources have stated that inorganic opportunities to acquire progressive organizations were considered but passed on. Instead, they waited until Pete and Gerry's and others were well on their way to exploding with national success across the Free Range, Free Range Organic, and Free Range Pasture Raised segment as noted in the Good, Better, and Best diagrams. The double-digit market sales were proven as covered in Chapter One of *Principles of Cartel Disruption* on value proposition and in Chapter Eight on early-stage milestones achieved.

The Laflamme business was a great innovator and success story. Controlling a large share of the overall distribution of the New England egg market for all eggs sold, Radlo Foods helped give Gerry and Jesse Laflamme their start. We assisted them with distribution and agreed to guarantee payments that aided with essential cash flow and security for their family survival and growth in the early years incubating Pete and Gerry's Organic and later Nellie's Cage Free. The assistance was in addition to the niche blue-green egg project that I was involved in at the Tufts veterinary school. Further, our in-store merchandising force had orders to ensure that their products were treated with the utmost integrity, aiding their sales efforts. Yes, we did not get paid on every case sold and, in fact, took some significant burns with customers that went out of business, but the Laflammes got a hundred cents on the dollar. I made sure of it. This action was against the urging of people in the industry. They wanted me to "put a nail in their coffin, David, once and for all!"

I follow a higher power, moral compass, and a steadfast desire to help others, and I have never regretted it. Some have said that it has been my greatest weakness. On the contrary, I believe it is my greatest strength in a purpose-driven life. They have accelerated further into $260M in revenue with 250 employees and working with 140 sustainable family farms with a very high enterprise value with premium prices. They were number one in Free Range and Free Range Organic. They have also expanded with additional pasture-raised shell offerings and into dairy with butter and processed items, including liquid eggs, hard-boiled eggs, and egg bites.

The announcement of a majority company sale to Butterfly in mid-year of 2021 will financially support their environmental and sustainable mission. CEO Jesse Laflamme said after growing the company 20–30% annually over this past decade that the company "has grown to a size that I honestly never could have imagined."[14]

Radlo Foods imagined great success with Certified Humane Free Range, Free Range Organic, and other high-end products, then incubated and accelerated them. We had the platform set for blockbuster success, just like the success from Eggland's Best with my partners. However, as John Bello, SoBe founder, former NFL Properties president, and Reed's chairman, said on my podcast, *Sustainable Leadership and Disruptive Growth* (davidradlo.com or your favorite podcast provider), "You need to have some luck sometimes."

Meanwhile, ExecThread CEO Joe Meyer, involved priorly at HopStop, acquired by Apple, and Quigo, acquired by AOL, said words to the effect that, "I was fortunate to have some crumbs left by the big player, Google," when he grew HopStop by 250% in revenue in two years with a whopping 500% in return on investment. When asked what the number one reason for their success was, in January of 2021 Laflamme told me that they were very lucky with how the big competition has behaved.

The New Eggland's Best "believes customers nationally only desire Eggland's Best and were in denial that customers would gravitate to socially conscious certified humane national brands." He thought they would have backed Born Free Certified Humane working with Radlo Foods, and he may have stayed a Northeast Regional brand until 2014. He also admitted that they were fortunate that Eggland's Best, including producers, did not acquire his company and brands previously during a short time between incubation and acceleration when they considered a sale about a decade ago. They benefited greatly from Radlo Foods' exit, the author's noncompete, and all that transpired after it.

The Born Free Certified Humane Free Range and Free Range Organic was an unusual situation. It's tough to attain a successful consumer product. But when you do, and it is growing at double-digit rates, it is rare for it to disappear from the shelves. It was an unusual situation throughout the Northeast for both Pete and Gerry's Cage Free and Pete and Gerry's Organic Cage Free to be right next to Certified Humane Born Free Free Range, Born Free Free Range Organic, and Born Free Cage Free. So when the Born Free Brand came off the shelf, it was a tremendous multimillion-dollar gift to them, as they immediately increased Certified Humane sales of his products to those same stores. They filled the gap where he did not have distribution and then quickly added the hard-boiled eggs and other products to fill in later. My exit was a defining moment for them.

They were able to switch to exclusive Free Range Certified Humane and Free Range Certified Humane Organic on their brands and fill in for Born Free's growing national Certified Humane Free Range penetration that customers were seeking. With the aid of my former national director of sales, Jim LeRoy, who was already wired into strategic planning, selling nationally for Born Free to the trade, and who also came with a pipeline and future targets setup, Pete and Gerry's could capitalize greatly on this opportunity. Showing their average growth plus Born Free growth turned into blockbuster numbers used as cash flow to fund national chain penetration coast to coast. The customer base was eager to take on their Certified Humane Free Range products. He added a second plant in Pennsylvania to support growth. As Tom Hanks noted in the movie *Forrest Gump,* he had a challenging time running a shrimping boat until a storm knocked out his competition: "After that, shrimping was easy," and so was blockbuster cash flow and accelerated enterprise value.

It's great that my neighbors, once close to bankruptcy, capitalized on the situation and hit a grand slam. It was painful to watch them sit on the bench. My former partners and their marketing management, the largest multi-billion-dollar group of producers that make up the New Eggland's Best cooperative, affiliated with a Fortune 500 company, refused to compete with these emerging segments effectively. The focus and support of Eggland's Best traditional lines had lapsed. They watched as socially progressive customers gravitationally "moved the goalposts" in wanting something "better" than cage-free that would become the replacement in the future for caged eggs.

Like Pete and Gerry's, successful efforts came to fruition by Mike Sencer and Tim Luberski, key management and owner of Hidden Villa, NestFresh, the Country Hen, and other lines. Former Eggland's Best team members Mike Culley, James Minkin, and "John John" Lombardi of CMC Food in New Jersey have grown in this progressive segment with their brand Farmer's Hen as well as private label in the Free Range, Free Range Organic and Free Range Pasture Raised premium segments. After a multi-decade-long relationship, sources have confirmed that CMC no longer ships nor represents Eggland's Best and their franchise owner-producers anymore.

In Canada, customers and great friends the Hudson and McFall families of Burnbrae Farms, led by Margaret, Ted, and Ian, with the spiritual inspiration of everyone's leader and mentor, Joe Hudson, have crushed it and continue to innovate and accelerate to this day with shell, liquid eggs, and egg product varieties. They are independently recognized for their management excellence. Chris Pierce of Heritage, Paul Kalmbach and family, and Wenger Feeds are all producers and feed companies servicing small family farms. The Kreider family deserves recognition for their new and clean facilities, growth in eggs, and diversification into humane dairy, iced tea, and emerging CBD products. The Sauder family focuses on quality shells and the Gibber family on liquid. John Brunnquell of Egg Innovations did well in the Midwest. Vital Farms is valued at around $1B, and Handsome Brook is holding its own. Cal-Maine recently acquired Happy Hen and is thriving.

Sustainability and environmental, social trends and governance (ESG) and progressive social action have been in for a segment of the market and an emerging new category. They have been sustainably benefiting many small producers throughout the supply chain from coast to coast. Further, local, sustainable family distributor Rich Mitlitsky of Mitlitsky Eggs in Connecticut, servicing the big markets of New England and New York, gained tremendously since our exit on various specialty items and commodity lines. Meanwhile, the Whaley family of Country Creek Farms in Bentonville, Arkansas, has dominated as a lead supplier to Walmart.

This is fabulous sustainable leadership, growth, and innovation by disrupting a cartel, accelerating, and maximizing performance, guys and gals! For market leaders, this lesson is what could happen and what you should do to not let it happen!

EXHIBIT: 8.B.   Retail (Non-Club and Military) Nielsen Numbers Before My Exit.

BY THE NUMBERS

For supermarket not including drug, mass merchants, military, and select club and dollar (nielson data ending September 1, 2012)

THEN - 2012

COMPANY	12 WEEKS REVENUE	52 WEEK REVENUE- ACTUAL/ACTUAL
	$ Sales	$ Sales
Eggland's Best	$116,156,352	$517,816,039
Land O'Lakes	13,020,687	$63,694,417
Born Free	$4,655,656	$18,474,877

NOW - 2020

COMPANY	12 WEEKS REVENUE	EXTRAPOLATED 52 WEEK REVENUE (based upon 4X plus 4 weeks sales)
	$ Sales	$ Sales
Eggland's Best	$234,734,000	$1,017,180,667
Land O'Lakes	16,232,121	$70,339,191

All Other EB Brands-Born Free II and others not available except as noted below Calmaine's acquired Happy Egg

The Happy Egg	$29,338,378	$146,691,890

ANALYSIS

As stated above, in the fall of 2012, plus a 25% approximate assessment of additional sales due to Walmart and other non-included retailers at the time in numbers in the above chart, would have equaled roughly $650,000 in 2012 more or less.

Eggland's Best has grown on a mature basis with its existing base SKU's. It is is still a very strong brand.

EXHIBIT 8.C.

Refrigerated & Frozen Foods buyer magazine for January/February 2021: You will find my analyzed comments below each brand and segment. It's turned into a multi-billion-dollar segmentation opportunity and emerging new category as noted in the prior Nielsen of Born Free, Free Range, Free Range Organic, and related products.

BY THE NUMBERS - 2020

FREE RANGE, FREE RANGE ORGANIC, AND FREE RANGE PASTURE RAISED:

COMPANY	12 WEEKS REVENUE $ Sales	EXTRAPOLATED 52 WEEK REVENUE (based upon 4X plus 4 weeks sales) $ Sales
PETE AND JERRYS	$34,357,810	$148,883,843
NELLIE'S	$29,392,341	$127,366,811
TOTAL PETE/ NELLIES Before		
PRIVATE LABEL, Pasture Raised, And Heirloom Eggs not included.	$63,750,151	$276,250,654

ANALYSIS

Gerry and Jesse Laflamme worked with us to distribute Pete and Gerry's in six packs to an industry leading company with enterprise value projected in the hundreds of millions of dollars approaching billions. They capitalized for further blockbuster growth backed by Butterfly Private Equity with the current COO, Eric Drake taking over as CEO. Great work Jim Leroy, Johnny Harris, Eric Puhacz, and Kevin O'Brien!

EXHIBIT 8.C.

BY THE NUMBERS - 2020

CMC'S FARMER HEN NOT LISTED

COMPANY	12 WEEKS REVENUE	EXTRAPOLATED 52 WEEK REVENUE (based upon 4X plus 4 weeks sales)
	$ Sales	$ Sales
VITAL FARMS: **** Handsome Brooke, Kreider Farms, and others not included.	$36,896,842	$159,886,315
OTHERS CMC'S FARMER HEN NOT LISTED		
Happy Egg Acquired by Calmaine Foods (now assumed to be an EB related Brand)	$29,338,378	$146,691,890

CATEGORY (BORN FREE GROWTH AREA)

Company Values are exceedingly high in this segment (category). Vital Farms (VITL), with approximately $160,000,000 in annual revenue as noted above on the high side, is valued at around $1B. Meanwhile, the largest owner-franchisee of Eggland's Best, Cal-Maine Foods (CALM), with approximately $1.4B in sales fluctuating based on commodity markets and growth, is valued at around $1.9B.

This figure is inclusive of property, plant, and equipment. The progressive sector generally buys eggs or leases bird production. The higher value is based on higher profit margins and higher rates of growth.

ANALYSIS

It's hard to believe that in close to a decade since the 50% acquisition of Eggland's Best by Land O'Lakes in 2012, this outstanding brand with tremendous brand equity has the same sales as it did a few months after paying $126M (Cal-Maine (CALM) and LOL publicly released financials).

That's a nice way of saying that it appears that the brand has been "shelved" from future significant growth and has had a White Space Major Opportunity Loss.

ANALYSIS

Based on credible sources, the CMC company sales are in the $100M to $120M range and are backed by a major international company positioned for growth. Great job Michael Culley, James Minkin, and "John John" Lombardi.

They were excited about the Born Free Certified Humane Free Range successes and quickly worked to fill in in many East Coast markets.

They have overcome their loss of Eggland's Best representation and distribution through the Metro New Jersey and New York area.

Let's get back to the time of my exit! Rose Acre Farms, who was not a small player by any means, sold their Eggland's Best franchise around the time I sold mine. CEO Marcus Rust and VP of Sales Greg Hinton of Rose Acre are outstanding producers and marketers nationally with brands like Allstar. Most recently, they are crushing it with Egglife, which are cage-free egg wraps and tortillas, among other significant innovations. They also maintained a minority interest in Opal Foods, based out of Missouri, which owns an Eggland's Best franchise according to information released by the prestigious agriculture investment firm AGR, headed by Ejnar Knudsen. AGR specializes in companies needing noncontrolling liquidity but will go into control if the situation is required. Recently, after a great ride in 2020, AGR sold their remaining interest in Opal to their partners, which included majority partner Tim Weaver of Weaver Bros. and Rose Acre Farms.

I planned to carry out my term at the American Egg Board after the sale of Radlo Foods. The United States secretary of agriculture appointed me to the position. The "powers that be" asked me to resign, which shocked me. The public appointment had nothing to do with Eggland's Best. It was involved with support of the federal government check-off programs in research, generic advertising, food service, and state and industry programs. I was on the American Egg Board for years as a board member and alternate board member. Rose Acre did not have these issues.

Senior Cal-Maine Foods executive Ken Looper was a legendary franchise owner and executive committee member. He used to say, "If you want to know strategic reasoning for rationale which may or may not make sense to you, 1. Watch! And 2. Find out what axes people have to grind."

According to public records in the US Patent Office, the New Eggland's Best owners, through their management, picked up the intellectual property of Born Free from an investment company that ran into capitalization issues and stopped operating. This happened several years after Eggland's Best management turned down interest in acquiring and partnering with Born Free Certified Humane and respecting the Land O'Lakes agreement that allowed us to continue to operate.

Rather than be the dominant category leader in Certified Humane Free Range, Free Range Organic in eggs and dairy, they saw the competition's coast-to-coast results. So they went into business as the late follower with Born Free II in eggs with new packaging on a region-by-region basis. This move was arguably the biggest strategic planning and execution blunder in consumer product marketing history and a lesson to those who want to fight progressive customer requests, sustainability, and environmental and social trends and governance (ESG), regardless of how big and powerful you are and how much distribution you control. The gravitational pull from the customer is king. The socially progressive market has grown so much that Free Range, Free Range Organic, and Free Range Pasture Raised may be classified as its own category now, distinct and different from other specialty eggs and products.

Unplanned Benefits to the Total Exit

I sold my business assets, the Born Free brand, partnership interest, and franchise in Eggland's Best after working 120 hours a week, at times, with no days off to build the specialty egg, dairy, food, export, and commodity businesses. Many partners benefited. It was a rollercoaster rocket ship ride from start to finish. Since I had my time back, I drove my daughter, Jess, to high school rowing practice. I took her to the Charles River in Boston to Community Rowing at 4:45 a.m. and then again at 3:00 p.m. I had the opportunity to help and spend time with my mom in the last years of her life.

Further, I could get to more Red Sox, Patriots, and Tufts Jumbo games with my son, Ben. The family finally got well-deserved time as I reintroduced myself to the golf club. I accelerated helping others succeed based upon my triumphs, failures, and everything in between, as well as giving back with time, talents, contacts, and finance.

PHOTO 7.A. *It is not important to mention everyone because Eggland's Best characterizes themselves similarly to the New England Patriots NFL franchise. The franchise is owned by fellow Tufts University sports alumni Danny Kraft, his dad Bob, his brother Jonathan, and his family. They have had their legendary run for decades as one TEAM: "Together Everyone Achieves More." I am in the second row, second from left.*

CHAPTER NINE

Local Country Club Cartel Disruption

Time to play golf—so I thought. The practice of golf club elitism and discrimination has been a way to maintain community power and control its market. Although the Civil Rights Act was signed in 1964 and there were other state statutes, private clubs were allowed to discriminate, exclude, and set quotas for members as long as they were strictly private. Many clubs chose to accommodate the public with room rentals, golf outings, functions, and lessons. The law has shown that they can't do such things if they are not strictly private. However, in a market setting, some clubs see discrimination as a right and a competitive advantage for their members that desire to be different, elite, and exclusive.

As noted, my dad was a decorated GI in Patton's army that liberated concentration camp survivors and accepted the surrender of two hundred German officers and soldiers. He came home from the war and finished his undergraduate degree at the University of Massachusetts and then graduate school at Iowa State University on the GI Bill. He played golf as often as possible in Iowa. However, when he came home to the Boston area, there were few if any clubs where he could play, so he gave up the sport. In his business, he did not solicit customers where these clubs functioned.

Country club discrimination has been going on for decades, if not centuries. Our longtime attorney and former NH District Court Judge Larry Warhall shared with me that when he grew up in the 1940s, he would drive with his grandparents and see signs alongside golf courses in Rhode Island and Massachusetts that said, "No Jews Allowed." In grammar school, he also recalled that a Jewish boy, a neighbor of mine, was routinely chastised before Easter. The boy was called a "Christ killer" and other derogatory phrases that traumatized him, so he left the school. Larry also said that he took lobbying trips in the 1980s with no other Jewish people in attendance. He ran into cutting remarks at the nation's capital by a publicly elected official that did not want to interact with Jewish people.

My grandfather, Mark Radlo, and his brother started Radlo Brothers in 1916. They were in the egg and poultry industry, and other brothers were in related food businesses. After working for a prominent Quincy Market food distribution company, the owner received flack from industry peers for needing two Jews to support their sales, so the brothers went out on their own.

In 1925, my grandfather became the token Jewish member of the Boston Fruit and Produce Exchange. In 1986, when I was running for Massachusetts state representative, I knocked on a door in a Boston suburb, where a man told me, "I am glad that you are running for office, David. We need a nice Italian boy like you to run. There are too many Jews in this town." Howie Carr, a prominent columnist, later cited the encounter in a *Boston* magazine article. Carr added, "Only one problem. Radlo is Jewish." And he was the nice one. But, unfortunately, not everybody was so courteous about it.

Today, we are in an exceedingly progressive era in terms of lack of tolerance for discrimination. In addition to an undergraduate degree from Tufts and a graduate degree from NYU Stern, I received an honorary degree from an outstanding Jesuit establishment, Boston College. I was always treated with tremendous respect and have the utmost reverence for the school, professors, and administrators.

We had a recreation swim and social membership at Sky Meadow Country Club, a beautiful golf and recreation facility in Nashua, NH. Ed Callahan was the general manager, and he ran it with his family. Jim Galletly is the fantastic senior executive that runs the membership and sales, and Rich Ingraham is the director of golf. You can find their website here: https://www.skymeadow.com. I consider it an affordable luxury. A group led by Rob Parsons recently acquired it. He is a local member and Sky Meadow community resident dedicated to making it an outstanding year-round recreation and dining destination. They also have great banquet facilities, a strong strategic business plan for growth, and an outstanding management team and associates. And Rob plans on scaling the club to new heights!

At the time, they offered and were willing to extend our membership to include golf for the entire family without issues. They graciously and sincerely appreciate our business. Sky Meadow is superior, with breathtaking views of mountains, natural water, and habitats. The club has won awards for its beauty, and I thoroughly enjoy playing golf there.

I owe a debt of gratitude to my customers, colleagues, and employees of the Christian, Muslim, and Buddhist faiths and other denominations that I have worked, played sports, and coached with over the years. So, when I inquired about and received an invitation to Nashua Country Club (NCC) to play golf and participate in a prospective member orientation and cocktail party, I was happy to accept the invitation with my girlfriend, now fiancée. My fiancée previously had done business with the club by booking an event and had purchased other small goods and services from them.

At the time, I wanted to check out NCC to play golf, see the facilities, and learn what they were about. They were putting in a curling rink, and they were interested in soliciting potential members and invited us to a prospective member orientation. The club perfectly staged the day. They had individuals on the new members' committee play golf with us and hosted a cocktail party that followed.

NCC came with other bells and whistles, including the increased social gathering of many professionals, the new curling rink, and activities like indoor golf. Most of all, the club was known for outstanding dining options and opportunities for social events. It was a year-round club that catered to all four seasons. They have had a competitive advantage in this arena, and this is New Hampshire, the "Live Free or Die" state. A good friend of mine was a member and suggested I check it out.

After several hours of getting to know my fiancée and me throughout the day, we were encouraged to complete an application. I asked a few questions of the membership director and then submitted the application.

Public Accommodation Facts

After surveying the NCC website, I noticed that they advertised their club on the same page as their public services. The Merrimack Valley Curling Club's website, which lists its official address in Lowell, Massachusetts, clearly states that it leases ice time from NCC.

There was a section that states, "NCC is committed to providing you and your guests with exceptional service, extraordinary facilities, and exquisite cuisine." It allows the public to fill in the information and explicitly lists functions like weddings, Bar Mitzvahs, reunions, showers, birthdays, anniversaries, fundraisers, charity events, golf tournaments, etc. NCC has a long history of public accommodations.

Expectations of Nondiscrimination

I expected that if the club had openings, they would not discriminate. After we applied in June, I received a call from the general manager and had some text exchanges. He wanted to schedule a meeting with the new members' committee to discuss membership. When I arrived at the meeting, there was a man I had played golf with from when I visited the club and a woman I hadn't met. The general manager and the membership committee posed several questions for me—none of the inquiries related to my ability to finance the membership fees. The manager told me NCC had the right to set quotas based on their designation as a private club. I was shocked that a club that provided public accommodations would overtly discriminate in such a fashion.

He asked me where I lived, and I explained that I resided most of the time in Nashua. I told them that I own real estate in Massachusetts and continue to pay Massachusetts state taxes as the commonwealth considers you a resident if you travel into the state for more than half of the year, including crossing the border to shop, work, travel, or get gas. If you are a former resident, you better keep a schedule and copious records, or the Massachusetts Department of

Revenue (DOR) will catch up with you. Mass DOR will fight to keep you as a dual resident! He stated that they did not want families joining separately to avoid two memberships.

They discovered that my domestic relationship did not meet their standard of traditional married couples. They moved on and steered away from any financial issues. From the questions I was asked, it seemed they only allowed a limited number of members from Massachusetts and monitored how many members they allowed from a divorced background or blended family. They also appeared to focus on the Jewish names on the application. I was surprised to be asked detailed questions like that because they publicly accommodate.

The committee members told me that I would hear back shortly before the Fourth of July. I contacted the general manager after we didn't hear back from the club. I let them know we were simply interested in playing golf, socializing, and patronizing the club. I received a written email stating, "The club didn't feel you would be a good fit." That's what the GM/COO of Nashua Country Club noted to us in a written email on July 18, 2017, as the reason why they turned us down for membership.

On July 20, 2017, I sent an email to the club's general manager to clarify why my girlfriend at the time and I were denied membership. I wanted to allow the club to be straight with us or apologize if they had made an error. Unfortunately, I have yet to receive an answer several years later. I felt there was alleged discrimination against us for at least marital reasons. Moreover, there was factual evidence to decide whether NCC had the right to do so, given their significant public accommodation and interstate commercial business.

Former New Hampshire District Court Judge Larry Warhall noted to me that if NCC stated to you that "the club didn't feel that you would be a good fit," it is a reasonable assertion that they are treating others similarly with alleged discriminatory factors. NCC may have quotas yet still reap the financial benefits of accommodating the public through other services. He encouraged us to challenge this action in whatever means possible, including contacting the state attorney general. He also suggested we consider filing a complaint with the New Hampshire Commission for Human Rights. Going to the media was also an option. I consulted my clergy and a key member of our congregation affiliated with the Anti-Defamation League (ADL).

Martin Luther King said, "Injustice anywhere is injustice everywhere." I am big on having people give facts up front, whether I want to hear them or not. NCC came into my cross hairs for not being straight and soliciting business without disclosing all terms and conditions. The club spent a lot of time and effort courting us. Al Pacino, acting as Tony Montana in *Scarface*, said, "I don't f-ck nobody that doesn't f-ck me first." My personal feelings are that if they want to discriminate, they should close down all of the accommodating services offered and be clear about who they are. They can offer all of these services to their members because they sell services to the public. In my estimation, they figured it would be best to maximize revenue by public accommodation and enact a private club with alleged discriminatory selection. This situation is similar to how there is tourist apartheid in Cuba, where exclusive services are afforded to a segment of the market to maximize tourism dollars through hotels and dollar stores. The goal is to maximize cash flow and member satisfaction.

The way I see it, NCC wanted to have an educated lesson on disrupting a local chapter of the country club cartel. So now they are getting one. First, I lobbied the state for action by filing a complaint with the Office of the Attorney General as recommended by Judge Warhall. It is a cost-effective method for the first pillar of disrupting the golf club establishment industry.

This situation is similar to advancing sustainability and de-commoditizing the egg industry with socially progressive cage-free, free-range, pasture-raised conventional, organic, and enhanced nutritional varieties. It relates to Martin Luther King Jr.'s progressive social action. The progressive model is the same whether it's the right for black and women's suffrage, women and minority rights to decrease the wealth gap, campaigns against the Vietnam War, equal rights for the LGBTQ community, or any other economic inequality, animal rights, or the march to zero-carbon equivalent emissions and environmental social governance. It would also apply to 50% of Americans who find themselves rebuilding after getting divorced, like my fiancée and our family. The process starts by utilizing laws, government relations, public relations or the threat of public relations, and court action to push the agenda forward. This action is like Dr. King's auspices and the Civil Rights Act of 1964 passed along with accompanying state laws.

From a business standpoint, clubs will fight anti-discriminatory practices because they feel the right to exclude anyone for any reason and set quotas as they see fit as long as they are private. Clubs will maximize their revenue in the silo with people that they choose to include. They also want to guard their revenue and community by doing business with the people that "fit in" best, which means in their heart of hearts, they have the right to discriminate while double-dealing on the public accommodation services to maintain their bottom line. It's like dealing with people in the dark without a spotlight operating one way and people with a spotlight on them utilizing another way. As Michael said to Sonny in the movie *The Godfather*, "It's not personal, Sonny, strictly business."

The inherent weakness with these clubs is decreasing membership revenue and finding alternate sources of income to offset operating costs. Hence, clubs like NCC accommodate the public to survive. When they make these accommodations, they are supposed to serve as a public operation and not discriminate for any reason. "Bad Boy" Jack DeCoster was quite philosophical about operating in the shadows. He said to me, "David, mankind cheats a little when no one's looking, yessiree, they do."

The Civil Rights Unit of the Office of the Attorney General caught NCC red-handed with alleged discrimination language weaved into their bylaws. The club was forced to strike such language and change its application to reflect that it will not discriminate. They were also instructed to get training in this regard. It's helpful when the law is on your side and you're willing to pursue it. In this case, New Hampshire law and federal civil rights laws supported the cause.

NH RSA 354-B:2 XIV states: Places of public accommodation include any inn, tavern, or hotel, whether conducted for entertainment, the housing or lodging of transient guests, or for the beneficial use of accommodations of those seeking health, recreation, or rest, any restaurant, eating house, public conveyance on land or water, bathhouse, barbershop, theatre, golf course, sports arena, health care provider, and music or another public hall, store or another establishment which caters or offers its services or facilities or goods to the general public. A public accommodation shall not include any institution or club which is in its nature distinctly private.

NCC previously maintained a domestic partner policy that prohibited unmarried couples from joining under a single membership unless the applicant and unmarried partner established:

They have chosen for at least two years to have continued to share their lives in a committed relationship that includes a mutual and exclusive commitment to each other.

They share the same permanent address.

They are jointly responsible for each other's common welfare; and

Financial interdependence.

This policy might have been retracted after recent events. Further, the application and membership guidelines specifically noted the word "spouse." This wording changed to "spouse/domestic partner." Their bylaws and membership handbook might have been revised as well. They have also agreed to add the following language to their membership application documents, including their current prospective member interview form, in boldface type, using letters of equal or greater size to those of the text in the body of the document: "NCC does not consider the age, sex, race, creed, or color, marital status, physical or mental disability, national origin, sexual orientation, or gender identity of an applicant, or any included spouse, significant other, and child during its membership application and evaluation process."

The attorney general alleged that the NCC's former domestic partner policy constituted discrimination based on marital status. Therefore, the policy would violate NH code 354-A if NCC was found to be a public accommodation rather than "distinctly private." You would think that they would want to make their best effort to get back to people they denied membership to to make amends per their agreement with the state and to do so within a few weeks after the agreement was signed because it is morally right. As "Bad Boy" Jack used to say, "In this world, when the light is shining on you after you get into a heap of trouble, you need to learn to be an expert at begging for forgiveness. Yessiree, you do!"

Then again, "Bad Boy" Jack went through a consumer and business boycott that cost him tens of millions of dollars in customer revenue that went swiftly to the competition in addition to massive regulatory scrutiny. Do you think Nashua Country Club could use similar encouragement?

On April 2, 2019, the club changed its membership policy for full and intermediate membership. "The full and intermediate categories are currently full to capacity, but we don't have a waiting list. However, during the last few years, openings have occurred during the summer, and we encourage you to apply. Associate Membership (under 30) has a three-year waiting list."

I will let you decide what you think of the April 2, 2019, policy. The assumption is that the policy may not make sense other than they may be looking for ways to take in an application, and if they are interested in the applicant for whatever reason, they will give them a call and let them in. If they are not interested, it's easy to say the club is full, so they are not accepting applicants. On April 2, 2019, perhaps the club was desperately grasping straws to maintain something that runs deep in their hearts and souls. They potentially wanted the ability to maintain an alleged cartel lock by being able to have a private club while keeping public revenues.

Notwithstanding, it takes a lot of guts to put this policy out while under a government consent order and continue to this day with the practice of "waiting lists." In fairness, they do have on their application the standard nondiscriminatory language that was placed into their material as compelled with a hammer by the attorney general of New Hampshire with their consent order.

In 2021, sources have confirmed that people went through the prospective member orientation. Allegedly, candidates from blended families similar to my situation and others that led to the New Hampshire Office of the Attorney General taking action against the club participated. Applicants were allegedly put on the "waiting list" after being "encouraged to apply" and having placed a deposit for the higher category segment (full, intermediate membership) as targeted by the April 2, 2019, policy. Apparently, now the applicants are placed on a "waiting list," but 2019 candidates were encouraged to apply without the waiting list option. This segment, a club within a club, needs to be guarded at all costs!

At the same time, the club, for marketing purposes, compared NCC with other clubs: "How is the club doing financially? May I see the financial reports for the past five years? Beware of the clubs that don't share that information. They may have bad news that they are hiding," NCC states on its website as of August 2021. This goes to the core of the successful dual public and private marketing segmentation practices, including their waiting list.

Throughout history, those that have experienced alleged club discrimination understand the secret code of the term "waiting list." The "waiting list" has been routinely used as a mechanism to disallow, limit, or delay certain population classifications to become members of clubs. Further, the club stated that as of "June 8, 2022" (I think they meant 2021), "Nashua Country Club is taking applications for memberships, but all membership categories are currently full, but they will be acted upon by September 1, 2021," and on September 7, 2021 stated "There is a multi-year waiting list for golf memberships." Really?

Further, it is important to ensure that candidates know that they may have been placed on the waiting list because their standing may be allegedly explicitly or implicitly suspect, with the cover that there is allegedly great demand and limited supply. NCC has done well with the way that they market and operate. As the club is pushing for full disclosure of other clubs, perhaps they should place on their website:

"Has the club operated under a consent order with New Hampshire's attorney general, who alleged discrimination?"

Full disclosure is the gracious country club and community service thing to do, especially for a club demanding full disclosure of their competition and also to honor Dr. Martin Luther King Jr., the state of New Hampshire, and the Civil Rights Act of 1964.

Full disclosure will also aid in previous, current, and new customers' analysis and allow them to review, reflect, and make an appropriate decision before agreeing to purchase club goods and services in light of their feelings and views about environmental, social governance (ESG), and alleged discrimination. You see, according to vocabulary.com, "To boycott means to stop buying or using the goods or services of a certain company or country as a protest; the noun boycott is the protest itself. The noun comes from Charles C. Boycott, an English land agent from 19th century Ireland who refused to reduce rents for his tenant farmers. As a result, the local residents did not want to have any dealings with him. Boycotts are an effective way to use your spending dollars to effect change."

Please read the attached consent order below in Exhibit 9.1., and I'll let you decide.

Exhibit 9.1. Assurance of Discontinuance Agreement between the New Hampshire Attorney General's Office and Nashua Country Club (received a copy of the agreement under the Right to Know Law on June 3, 2021).

ASSURANCE OF DISCONTINUANCE

1.   The State of New Hampshire, by and through its attorneys, accepts this Assurance of Discontinuance following its investigation of Nashua Country Club's ("NCC") membership policies pursuant to the New Hampshire Law Against Discrimination, RSA 354-A.

2.   The parties have voluntarily agreed, as indicated by the signatures below, to resolve the allegations against NCC without the necessity of litigation or a trial on the merits. There has been no finding of any violation of law, and NCC expressly denies that it is a place of public accommodation as defined by RSA 354-A:2, XIV, that it has discriminated against membership applicants based on marital status, or that it has otherwise violated RSA 354-A.

3.   The Attorney General makes no finding as to whether NCC is a place of public accommodation, whether any violation of law occurred, or whether any discrimination took place.

Parties

4.   Pursuant to RSA 354-A, the Attorney General may file complaints with the New Hampshire Commission for Human Rights ("Commission") to allege violations thereof. In connection with the filing of such a complaint, the Attorney General may take proof, issue subpoenas, and administer oaths in the manner provided in the civil practice law and rules.

5.   NCC is a 501(c)(7) corporation that operates a private country club, which offers sports facilities and restaurants to its members.

Applicable Law

6.   RSA 354-B:17 states in relevant part:

> It shall be an unlawful discriminatory practice for any person, being the owner, lessee, proprietor, manager, superintendent, agent or employee of any place of public accommodation, because of the age, sex, race, creed, color, marital status, physical or mental disability or national origin of any person, directly or

1

indirectly, to refuse, withhold from or deny to such person any of the accommodations, advantages, facilities or privileges thereof . . .

7.   RSA 354-B:2, XIV states:

"Place of public accommodation" includes any inn, tavern or hotel, whether conducted for entertainment, the housing or lodging of transient guests, or for the benefit, use or accommodations of those seeking health, recreation or rest, any restaurant, eating house, public conveyance on land or water, bathhouse, barbershop, theater, golf course, sports arena, health care provider, and music or other public hall, store or other establishment which caters or offers its services or facilities or goods to the general public. "Public accommodation" shall not include any institution or club which is in its nature distinctly private.

Allegations of Fact

8.   The Attorney General alleges that NCC is a place of public accommodation as defined by RSA 354-B:2, XIV.

9.   NCC previously maintained a now-retracted domestic-partner policy that prohibited unmarried couples from joining pursuant to a single membership, unless the applicant and unmarried partner established:

> a.   They have chosen, and for at least two years have continued to, share their lives in a committed relationship that includes a mutual and exclusive commitment to each other;
>
> b.   They share the same permanent address;
>
> c.   They are jointly responsible for each other's common welfare; and
>
> d.   Financial interdependence.

At all times, this policy was applied uniformly, regardless of sexual orientation.

10.   The Attorney General alleges that NCC's (now former) domestic-partner policy constituted discrimination based on marital status, and therefore, the policy would violate RSA 354-A if NCC was found to be a public accommodation rather than a "distinctly private" entity.

2

RTK 000002

11.   The Attorney General could have filed a charge of discrimination with the New Hampshire Commission for Human Rights, alleging that NCC is a public accommodation and that its domestic-partner policy violates RSA 354-A. Instead of pursuing such an action, the parties have entered into this Assurance of Discontinuance, pursuant to which the parties agree as follows:

Membership Policy

12.   NCC has adopted a policy establishing the process by which members may add a spouse/domestic partner to their membership. This policy establishes that marital status is not a consideration. The new policy, "Membership of Spouse/Domestic Partner," is attached as **Exhibit A**.

13.   NCC has revised its bylaws and membership handbook to include the policy contained in **Exhibit A.**

14.   NCC has removed its former domestic-partner policy from its bylaws and membership handbook.

15.   NCC has revised its bylaws and membership handbook to replace each reference to "spouse" with "spouse/domestic partner."

16.   NCC has added the following language to its membership application documents, including its current "Prospective Member Interview" form, in bold-face type using letters of equal or greater size to those if the text in the body of the document:

> NCC does not consider the age, sex, race, creed, color, marital status, physical or mental disability or national origin, sexual orientation, or gender identity of an applicant, or any included spouse, significant other, and/or child during its membership application and evaluation process.

3

17.   NCC has added the following language to the main page of its website, as well as to the "Membership" and "How to Join" pages, in bold-face type using letters of equal or greater size to those if the text in the body of the document:

> NCC does not consider the age, sex, race, creed, color, marital status, physical or mental disability or national origin, sexual orientation, or gender identity of an applicant, or any included spouse, significant other, and/or child during its membership application and evaluation process.

If NCC subsequently revises or reorganizes its website, it agrees to include this language on all pages related to applying for membership at NCC.

Membership Applications

18.   Within fifteen (15) days of execution of this Agreement, NCC agrees to identify any and all applications for membership or applications to add a domestic partner to an existing membership that were denied, in whole or in part, because of the former domestic-partner policy. NCC will re-evaluate such application(s) and, if appropriate under NCC's membership standards, grant membership.

Training

19.   NCC has notified employees and members that it has revised its membership policy as relevant to spouses/domestic-partners. NCC has posted an electronic copy of the revised policy on its website, and has posted on its information bulletin board a notice of the update and the web address where it may be found online.

20.   Although NCC disputes that it is a public accommodation, the organization is committed to the principles of equal opportunity. To that end, NCC seeks to ensure that its membership application and interview process complies with New Hampshire Law Against Discrimination and Title VII of the Civil Rights Act of 1964.

4

RTK 000004

21.   As such, NCC agrees to take certain steps to ensure that members and volunteers who conduct prospective-member interviews are educated about non-discrimination. The steps to be taken, as set forth below, are designed in consideration of the fact that NCC relies upon wide array of members and volunteers to conduct prospective-member interviews, including Board members, Committee member, and also general members. Therefore, within ninety (90) days of the execution of this Agreement, NCC will implement a three-tier system to ensure that interviewing techniques comply with the New Hampshire Law Against Discrimination and Title VII of the Civil Rights Act of 1964:

    a.   Within ninety (90) days of the execution of this Agreement, NCC will provide live anti-discrimination training to members of management who are directly involved in the membership process (David Scaer, General Manager/COO and the Membership Coordinator), the Chairs of the Membership and the Membership Development Committees, and two (2) additional Committee members who actively participate in prospective-member interviews. This training shall address, but need not be limited to, the New Hampshire Law Against Discrimination, Title VII of the Civil Rights Act of 1964, and interviewing techniques that comply therewith. NCC agrees to bear the cost of this training.

    b.   On or before January 30, 2020 and January 30, 2021, NCC will provide a refresher training course to the above named individuals (or their replacements, in the event of a change in management or Chair position).

    c.   Within ninety (90) days of the execution of this Agreement, NCC will create an interview information packet containing the new policy identified as **Exhibit A**; the statement of non-discrimination referenced in paragraphs 16 and 17, above; a

5

RTK 000005

document outlining proposed interview questions; and a document outlining the types of questions that may not be asked in an interview.

d. Prior to each prospective-member interview, one of the two (2) above-named management employees (or their replacements) will transmit the interview information packet to the assigned interviewer(s), together with an oral or written reminder to review the policy, proposed questions, and prohibited questions prior to each interview. The trained employees and Committee Chairs will make themselves available to address any questions from prospective interviewers about these materials.

Reporting Requirements

22. NCC agrees, no later than fourteen days after the occurrence, it will provide the Attorney General with notice and documentation of completion of each act required pursuant to this Assurance of Discontinuance.

23. NCC agrees to provide notice to the Civil Rights Unit at the New Hampshire Department of Justice, for a period of three (3) years, of any membership application that is denied based on marital/domestic partner status. In the event that such a denial occurs, NCC agrees to provide the Civil Rights Unit at the New Hampshire Department of Justice with on-site access to its membership records.

24. NCC agrees to provide the Civil Rights Unit at the New Hampshire Department of Justice, for a period of three (3) years, with on-site access to its records for the purpose of ensuring NCC's compliance with this Assurance of Discontinuance.

Entry and Duration

6

RTK 000006

25.   This Assurance of Discontinuance shall be in effect for a period of three years from the date of entry.

26.   This Assurance of Discontinuance shall not be construed as an admission of violation for any purpose, but if a court determines that there has been a violation of any of the terms of this Assurance of Discontinuance, the Attorney General may seek civil penalties pursuant to RSA 354-A and/or such other remedies as may be provided by law.

27.   The Attorney General has reviewed the NCC's revised domestic-partnership policy. However, this Assurance of Discontinuance shall not be construed as a statement or guarantee that any NCC policy or practice, including those referenced herein, comply or fail to comply with state or federal law, including RSA 354-A.

Additional Provisions

28.   This Assurance of Discontinuance shall be binding upon and inure to the benefit of NCC's successors and assigns. Actions or inactions of NCC's officers, directors, contractors, agents and employees, acting under or for NCC, involved in the implementation of this Assurance of Discontinuance shall be considered actions or inactions of NCC.

29.   The Attorney General reserves all legal and equitable remedies, sanctions, and penalties that might be available to enforce the provisions of this Assurance of Discontinuance.

30.   The parties acknowledge that NCC, its successors and assigns, have a continuing obligation to remain in compliance with all applicable laws and rules. The Attorney General reserves the right to bring administrative, civil and/or criminal enforcement action for any violation of state and federal anti-discrimination laws relating to any new facts or allegations and arising after the date that the parties signed this Assurance of Discontinuance.

7

31.   In the event that either party must initiate a legal action to enforce the terms of this Assurance of Discontinuance, the prevailing party shall have the right to collect from the other party its reasonable costs and attorneys' fees incurred in enforcing this Assurance.

32.   The Attorney General's failure to enforce any provision of this Assurance after any breach or default shall not be deemed a waiver of its rights with regard to that breach or default, nor shall such failure be construed as a waiver of its right to enforce each and all of the provisions of this Assurance upon any further breach or default.

Agreed to and approved by:

Gordon J. MacDonald
Attorney General

Date: 11/29/18

Elizabeth A. Lahey, NH Bar No. 20108
Assistant Attorney General, Civil Rights Unit
Office of the Attorney General
33 Capitol Street
Concord, NH 03301

Date: 11-26-18

David Scaer, Authorized Agent
Nashua Country Club
25 Fairway Street
Nashua, NH 03060

8

RTK 000008

CHAPTER TEN

The Secret and Hidden 12th Principle: Understand the Cartel
Leadership Rules

(Official and Unofficial Version)

At times, cartels use written or unwritten rules to function. They enforce the rules to maximize profit and cash flow and, at times, preserve dominance and order. Below, I will introduce you to some common methods used by cartels for control and order. Whether you are a disruptor, sustainable leader, a dominant market leader, or a cartel leader, you need to be aware of the basic rules and those that may specifically pertain to your industry or geographic area.

Some of these rules are general descriptive realities in the US but may not be legal. I am not an attorney and would advise that you get appropriate legal advice before implementing any of these in your industry or organization. As a disruptor, you should know that these items may be happening in the area you are operating, so you should have your eyes wide open as you plan and go to market. In Chapter Four of *Principles for Cartel Disruption*, I discuss that basing strategies on a flawed set of assumptions can result in disaster.

Rule 1) Discuss Pricing and Coordinating Market and Supply Action: Discuss market prices with competitors and then coordinate actions to reduce supply or take actions jointly to increase market demand to force price increases.

Rule 2) Control Pricing: Control the price charged to customers and take advantage of situations in the market to utilize a competitive advantage to increase your profit. Reduce advertising or promotion costs or take action to drive category market share, profits, and volume.

Rule 3) Never Miss an Opportunity: When supply is short or there is a crisis that causes a spike in demand, you may choose to band together and ensure that price increases, profits, and cash flow are maximized. You can reduce prices later when supply increases or unforeseen demand diminishes.

Rule 4) Control Supply or Output: An example of controlling the supply or output is when the oil cartel, OPEC, manages oil prices through supply cuts or increased output.

Rule 5) Give Kickbacks to Owners and Key Parties for Following the Rules and Receiving Results: Either privately or aboveboard, reward the organization or government for maintaining or increasing dominant market share, profits, and other critical indicators set by the cartel through the ones in control.

According to *Havana Nocturne: How the Mob Owned Cuba . . . and then Lost It to the Revolution,* the Cuban mob made sure they passed profits to key financial stakeholders and government officials in the Batista regime. I also had fiery discourse with Fidel Castro about the matter. If possible, reward the rule-abiding owners and key parties such as executive management by taking resources from the ones that break the rules in every possible way. It's only fair.

Rule 6) Understand the Real Consequences of Engaging with the Cartel: If you don't obey the rules, you can lose kickbacks, be terminated or pushed out of business or even worse!

Rule 7) Discriminate with Your Membership Selection: Bring people in that you like and see fit. Cartel Leadership will turn down those that they don't want. The goal is to maximize revenue and increase cash flow.

Rule 8) Control the Four P's: Control price, promotion, place (distribution), and product (service).

8A) Distribution Restraints: Use restraint on the ability to distribute competitive services or products using whatever means necessary unless the cartel works a deal out to get paid on competitive services or products or receives an option to buy out the competition. Remember, eliminate or work with the competition and increase cash flow.

8B) Use Whatever Means Necessary to Control Market and Sales Restraints: Seek to increase the market scope and decrease the amount of competition that sells services or products to regions and specific customers. The cartel will be enriched and control the marketing, sales of the existing category, and new service or product offerings, and competition selling to accounts. This situation would extend to third-party vendors, salespeople, brokers, distributors, and other extended family members as a means of loyalty and to carry out the cartel's mission.

8C) Pricing:

8C1) Base Control: Control the Price if Appropriate by Using a Cartel Salesforce: Work to eliminate as much competition on buying service or product customers as possible that hurts profits, margins, and cash flow.

8C2) Control the Territory: Work with the friendly cartel members or competition to lower rates to drive smaller capitalized competitors out of business. The goal is to eliminate the competition and increase cash flow. Raise your rates after the competition is out of business based on a buyout or a go-out.

Rule 9) Financially Fight Disrupting Competitive Influences Singularly or Jointly: Don't fight fair! Bury the competition with a disproportionate amount of spending in the form of pricing reductions, incentives, incremental slotting or listing fees for services or goods, and other advertising and promotions where they are focused. Kill their test markets in both traditional and new public relations and digital marketing venues. Large companies will use this method. According to former Kellogg executive and NYU Stern Professor Mike Darling, who is now at Queen's Smith School of Business in Canada, you need to spend about three times more on your launch with a new brand than one that's established. Fighting early on is very important to defend your brand, services, and products.

Per Chapter 8 of *Principles of Cartel Disruption,* to accelerate and maximize performance disruptors, use operational metrics to guide your early-stage growth and milestone targets. It usually takes eighteen months for the large competitors to wake up. Sometimes the cartel or large company will get wind and be right in a disruptor's face with a competitive reaction.

Rule 9A) Use Sophisticated Analytical Information and Move *around* Intellectual Property (IP): A Derby Entrepreneurship Center at Tufts colleague of mine, Peter Clay, is a former senior executive at Gillette. He was responsible for the launch of many Gillette razors and products, including the Sensor. He explains this principle well in his advisory work with Jack Derby, Tina Weber, Dean Kevin Oye, and Dean Chris Swan. Cartels and large corporations may have mega-resources, with the ability to be sophisticated, organized, and targeted, with the best analytical information and portfolio information to defend and strike back and jointly work on changes to competitive situations or environmental or social trends.

With regard to intellectual property, find legal ways around existing patents filed in similar ways through different patents and trade secrets. For disruptors, understand that big competitors may just steal or attempt to steal your novel art and/or technology if they can and have you fight them in court with resources you may not have. This is why sometimes it is a better route to go with a trade secret than filing for patent protection.

Rule 10) Audit Tollbooth Kickbacks to the Cartel: Ensure that the cartel gets paid appropriate kickbacks on all or most services, products, and vendor services or supplies sold to cartel members on official or unofficial cartel-related services or products. "Bad Boy" Jack DeCoster said, "The problem with mankind is when people steal a little, it usually leads to them stealing a lot, yessiree, it does." Or as President Reagan used to say, "Trust but verify." Bring in the bean counters!

Rule 11) Extend the Reach and Influence of "The Family": Extend the reach to nonexclusive service or product distributors through kickback requirements. This process can be done directly or with a bigger upcharge on service or products handled or transported for competitive products; or require exclusivity to keep the business. The cartel can leverage down their dominance and market power to increase profitability and the cost of doing business for the competition. If service or product distributors are disloyal, termination and cease and desist orders may need to be issued using mechanisms to weaken and punish their disloyalty.

Rule 12) Strategically Roll Up and Acquire: Make the Most of Your Inorganic Acquisition Activity: A cartel, private-equity-backed firm, or dominant strategic partner can eliminate the competition and increase cash flow through acquisition. With fewer boats in the water, you can charge more and have greater processing efficiencies for additional cash flow. Use your dry powder to roll up and acquire! And don't be penny-wise and pound-foolish!

Internally for cartel owners and senior management, please be wise and judicious in executing the common enemy strategic approach (retribution) of members that take advantage of disrupting niche customer segments the cartel hasn't embraced yet. The cartel's lifeblood is from kickbacks or tribute revenue to the cartel from product or service revenue. Don't destroy customer-segmented markets when they appear. Buy them or strategically work with them to satisfy new customers' needs and wants.

Successful customer growth segments are ever emerging, and you may not be tuned in to them as you accelerate and manage a large, growing organization. Be careful of people internally focusing on carrying out the cartel mission and chopping down trees with blinders on while forgetting to review the strategic forest landscape. Get a tall fire engine ladder, a spotlight, or climb up into the forest ranger's tower. Many can't see the strategic forest because the trees are in the way. Don't let that be you and your organization!

At this point, you must have board members to hold your management accountable for their actions. I discuss the importance of board members in Chapter Ten of *Principles for Cartel Disruption.* You don't want a bunch of yes-people. It can cause massive disruption to your services or product cartel and may cost you financially. It is also essential to have different strong points of view when disrupting and accelerating growth!

When you choose to sell your business, realize that selling a company has its own industry of investment bankers, venture capitalists, buyer debt and equity finance professionals—trusted advisors to prepare and drive your value to the highest level. Part of what I do is help companies and executives get ready for the sale and bring in the correct firms to finance the project. The buy-and-sell game is an industry on its own. Beware!

Rule 13) Have a Dispute Resolution System for Cartel Members: Ensure that there is a formal or informal process to resolve any issues among members concerning competitive activity and appropriate compensatory settlement. Avoid fighting for market share, distribution, and revenue-based business that may drive down prices and cash flow for the greater good of all cartel members.

Rule 14) Get Government Blessings and Cooperation because it Gives You an Advantage: If you can get the government to bless or endorse your actions, good for you. The mob had a willing partner with Batista in Cuba, but not so much with Castro, who ran his own island. In the US, it is a bit subtler than that. Many industries are exempted from antitrust laws. Although there are active criminal antitrust, racketeer influenced and corrupt organizations (RICO) investigations and prosecutions, there are not the same level of incentives on RICO/antitrust whistle-blowers.

There are tax statutes where people can bring forth information to the IRS and state authorities and get a piece of the settlement. Therefore, there is no incentive for people with information to turn evidence over to the government except for being a patriotic citizen. Congress has resisted enacting incentives to whistle-blowers on antitrust issues in private enterprises. Do you think private company associations have lobbied Congress on this?

Rule 15) Alternate Rule: Informal Communication Is Better because Loose Lips Sink Ships: Another option is to keep it informal. It's not foolproof, but operating in this manner is the least risky and best for all involved. Former New York prosecutor Eliot Spitzer said, "Never talk when you can nod, and never nod when you can wink, and never write an email because it's death. You're giving prosecutors all the evidence that we need." There is an industry of attorneys suing companies for collusion and other antitrust activities.

Philosophical and Historical Thoughts:

The foundation of the United States government and many other forms of government originates from the principles of democracy based on Thrasymachus and Harrington, where statutory law passes by dominant interest groups in society and politics flow from economics. Hedrick Smith, in his book *The Power Game: How Washington Works*, points out directly how Washington, DC, works.[15] Industry lobbies heavily against enacting incentives on whistle-blower antitrust laws. The big funder, John Hancock, got his first position on the Declaration of Independence. So, continue to do as Benjamin Franklin said when signing: "Hang together."

If the union comes looking for you, remember there was one surviving member of Mary Surratt's gang that did not "hang together" with her courtesy of the Union Army. Mary Surratt was involved in the conspiracy to kill President Abraham Lincoln shortly after the Civil War. President Lincoln's assassination took place on April 15, 1865, at Ford's Theatre in Washington, DC. Mary's son John, a Confederate courier and spy, and his friend John Wilkes Booth were accused of attempted kidnapping and conspiracy to murder Abraham Lincoln. Mary's son ran like hell to Canada, Europe, and Egypt and served briefly as a Pontifical Zouave. By the time the authorities tried to extradite him, the statute of limitations had expired. He lived a long and fruitful life.

Alternatively, some have chosen to head down where it's warm to Cuba or other places where you won't be extradited, as noted earlier with my questions to Fidel Castro on New Jersey's JoAnne Chesimard. The mojitos, *siete anos* rum, Habanos, and Churchills are pretty good. *Huevos* and *pollo* (eggs and chicken) are not bad when they have them in stock.

If you go to Varadero Beach to do business, they have cartel segmentation practices in play with exclusive areas for international tourists and businesspeople, as Pennsylvania's Ron Kreider and Export Council members observed. The military will serve you drinks in flowery shirts along with appropriate entertainment.

Then again, perhaps reflect on those British soldiers involved in the Boston Massacre that were wise enough to hire arguably the best legal mind in American history, later our second president, John Adams. In Chapter Three of *Principles of Cartel Disruption,* I discuss attaining a modern-day John Adams-like former federal prosecutor, Joe Savage. "He is the smartest 'misunderstanding' white-collar-crime criminal lawyer in the United States," according to Kevin Cloherty, deputy general counsel of Manulife-John Hancock and former head of the New England Organized Crime Strikeforce. (Kevin worked for Joe.)

I will stand behind former Massachusetts Bar President Chris Kenney of Kenney & Sams; and former Brooklyn ADA Rob Friedman and his partner, antitrust attorney Dan Brown of Sheppard Mullin. I also endorse the brightest corporate law minds of Kitt Sawitsky, Greg Getschman, and "tough guy litigator" Alan Reisch of Goulston & Storrs and seasoned tough local counsels like Josh Brown of Branford, CT, and Captain Brian McGrail of Wakefield, MA. For IP litigation, Doug Kline and Sam Ibrahim are the best. Jose Casal and Raul Cosio in Miami are tops. Meredeth Beers is the best planning, trusts, and estate attorney known, to make sure you don't lose it all playing poker and shooting craps.

They will take care of bringing in the specialists and bill you until the chickens come home to roost. Except for Josh and Brian, I swear that at times when Chris sees a great case, he's willing to take it on contingency. You see, the Good, Better, and Best value proposition I noted in Chapter One of *Principles of Cartel Disruption* applies to legal fee services positioning as well, which was confirmed by Catherine "Cathy" Woodward Gill, an expert in legal administration. Listen to what the attorneys tell you to do, admit no wrongdoing, and work out misunderstandings amicably. Hell, put on attorney Chris Kenney's wedding ring if you can't dismiss the darn baseless nonsense, and roll the dice at trial if the attorneys recommend such.

With time, money, and lawyers, you never know. You just may come out the winner! If you don't win, take a page from "Bad Boy" Jack DeCoster. Cut a deal with decent money to settle or become an expert at begging for forgiveness. Plead, "Judge, I swear I am sorry." Then, overly pay restitution for misunderstandings. Then, perhaps reframe and see the benefits of a few months in a country club prison to pray, cleanse your soul, and help others; if the country club lets you in! Just make sure along the way you use your vast resources to give back to transform for a safer, new, and better world.

Lessons Learned for Cartel Disruptors:

Keep your eyes wide open as you put these conditions in your plan. John Bello says, "It's a tough world out there." Bello put his house on the line with SoBe, and it wasn't an immediate success, as he needed to make changes to the packaging, design, and product. He says he "got lucky" on distribution and some key athlete endorsements.

When the going gets tough, think about George Washington. He was outnumbered without resources and surrounded by the British Army. I went through several failures myself. I shared earlier in this book about the mistakes I made with the shipping business. Also, it took a few relaunches of specialty eggs to find success. Even Eggland's Best was initially called Heartland's Best, which regulators turned down. For Eggland's Best, the slogan "Now You Can Eat Real Eggs Again" attained regulatory scrutiny. It took a few relaunches to finally get out of the test stage and develop the Good, Better, and Best framework in specialty eggs. The concept was not an overnight success. It took a lot of work to incrementally improve the packaging, product, marketing, messaging, trade force, production quality specifications, support technology, and full partner support. Due to the regulatory scrutiny, it cost much more than previously projected to get off the ground.

You can also reflect on what Castro said to me that I shared earlier in this book. He recalled waiting with a few soldiers in the Sierra Maestra Mountains. He shared the lessons that he learned from the South losing to the North at

Gettysburg and the strategic advantage of being based in the mountains.

When you engage with a person or entity, uncover their character. From my experience, honest and generous people bring about better outcomes seconded by someone who is honest but cheap. If you get thrust into a situation where someone is dishonest but generous, you can still work through issues and move on with a great attorney if you choose; but I would suggest staying away from anyone who is dishonest and cheap under most, if not all, circumstances. The dishonest person will burn you in the end. Inc. 5000 company International Products Group CEO Bob Goehrke, as noted by a former board member of mine, quickly says, "Don't do business with jerks." Perhaps Dr. Bob learned that prophecy at Harvard Business School. Adam Grant of Wharton says people are "Givers, Takers, and Matchers."[16] Meanwhile, my editor, Carolyn Olson, says, "Sever relationships that do not align with your vision, morals, and values."

Most importantly, all success is not measured economically. As noted in Chapter Five of *Principles of Cartel Disruption*, you need to find out what motivates you and your team. This process can be done through quick psychographic and organizational research. Find your blind spots so you can locate anyone not taking the right action to reframe and transform your results. Success will come when you understand and follow the cartel rules, along with the other eleven *Principles of Cartel Disruption,* in order to sustainably transform for a Safer, New, and Better World.

AFTERWORD

When you enter the business world, focus on taking the right action. Be open to learn and appreciate all of the lessons you receive, even the challenging ones. Always strive to improve your results. In the process, find time to give back and enjoy your life!

You may end up owning, managing, or being part of an organization that will last a hundred or more years. You may sell your business for a premium or a discount. Depending on the circumstances, you may have to take the "f-ck you" money you deserve if a cartel forces you out. You could become a dominant player or have the opportunity to free some prisoners. If you are lucky, you will help change the lives of many or lead a nation.

It's your life. How you determine success and your right action utilizing your value proposition, funding, operational excellence, sustainability, and giving back to transform for a safer, new, and better world is what genuinely matters. As Warren Buffett said in his letter to shareholders in 2015, "Much of what you become in life depends upon whom you choose to copy and admire."[17] So whom did I choose to learn from?

I am still on a learning journey, but first and foremost, I learned from my customers. As noted in Chapter Ten in *Principles of Cartel Disruption*, "Accelerate and Maximize Performance," my comparative skill set rock star board was a team of outstanding specialists. Seeing them in action was a great experience. My competition deserves mention because these forces drive excellence. Competition always drives you to excel at all 12 Principles to satisfy customers and markets, or, of course, they would be happy to take care of them for you.

I give appreciation to Jim Elliott, the late WWII hero and political philosophy professor at Tufts University, in my formal education. He gave great respect and deference to multiple viewpoints. Professor Brad Seasholes taught me to respect and appreciate the people that give you opportunities. He also did one hell of an impersonation of Richard Nixon when he left the White House. Mike Darling from NYU Stern and Queen's College deserves mention for teaching how to create, finance, and lead just like he did at Stern courtesy of the Kellogg Company.

Head Sports Coaches

Bill Tighe was a legendary high school football coach in America. He was the longest-serving high school coach, and I had the opportunity to be one of his players and then later in life coach with him. He taught how to mold young athletes into confident, strong, tough leaders and win at football, family, and life. Tufts coaches Vic Gatto, Duane Ford, John Casey, and Ed Gaudiano taught inspirational growth and a success mindset that acknowledged losing but never seeing the loss as failure. They taught me how to smile, laugh, and be tough at the same time. Line coaches Joe Lopresti, John Sullivan, and Mike Brown provided essential toughness and fun inspiration.

Corporate Training Ground Folks

Craig Frischling and John Briare of Citicorp and Ken Kraetzer, Steve Eulie, and Lois Deming from Chase deserve mention in all things excellent basic training in consumer products marketing, both classic and direct response, sales, and operational flow. Most recently, I am appreciative to Trusted Advisor coaches and consultants Rick Lochner, Doug Brown, Arnie Rintzler, Paul Anovick, Gerard Mott, Tammy Kohl, Jenna Moll, and Wendy Howland for giving one heck of a management consulting and executive coaching education, post exits. Mike Jeans and the late Clint Allen from the American College of Corporate Directors (ACCD) also deserve mention for an outstanding board education. Sharpen that saw!

Also, appreciation goes to the venture, private equity, and investment banking folks such as Sam Bartlett of Charlesbank, Ted Tutun of Stifel, and Gary Domoracki of Oppenheimer, where I learned from working on both the buy and sell side of mergers, acquisitions, and investments. I wish all of the $2.3B deals I've worked on hit, but I'm delighted some of them did. Ben Carson Jr. and Harrison Perry, founding partners of Interprise and Fvlcrum, have shown how to disrupt and accelerate their outstanding niche in private equity and bring back blockbuster 9.3X returns quickly! And give back more! Investigate why people think the way they do. Seek to understand before being understood.

Liberals, Moderates, and Conservatives

I had a unique education learning from Republicans, Democrats, liberals, moderates, conservatives, and then Communist-Socialists by way of Fidel Castro. Dr. Martin Luther King called it "loving your enemies." Sustainable leadership and constructive engagement start with an intense ability to understand what people you may not agree with think and why they reflect on matters the way they do to build bridges for the future. New England is a special place where we have the town meeting mentality of working together, solving issues, and going home. We try to impart our theory of working together in a civil, gracious, and respectful manner for the common good.

I worked for or did business with the following people: first, from right to left on the political spectrum, I worked for Jeff Jacoby, a conservative Republican, on the US senatorial campaign of a very conservative business owner. Jeff is now with the *Boston Globe* to share his conservative intelligence. The campaign manager at the time, Joe Malone, is a friendly but tough Republican leader. However, I am still afraid of Joe's wife after an incident of mistakenly taking the former Massachusetts treasurer's suitcase from the carousel after a return flight from the 1988 Republican National Convention. My roommate in New Orleans, Dan "Dots" Doherty, believed that the suitcase might have been his. I let it sit weeks before meeting with Dots to verify. My mind was on my credit and debit cards that had been stolen on the last night of the convention. Joe was in the middle of a US senatorial campaign against the late Democratic Senator Ted Kennedy and was left short on clothes due to my mishap.

I appreciate my state representative campaign and later company advisor Ron Mills, who taught me the art and science of messaging to different segments. He also developed "El Mappe" for Cuban development with Castro. Former Massachusetts Republican head, legislator, and State Department senior diplomat Andrew Natsios was a key mentor who expected early days and late nights of work from me. In exchange, he provided me with great opportunities to succeed, network, and meet transformative leaders. Through him, I met President and Vice President George H. W. Bush, who publicly characterized me, the sustainable leader and cartel disruptor, as "articulate." I also was introduced to other presidential candidates through functions and networks.

Andrew led efforts to stop ethnic cleansing in Darfur as a special ambassador after serving stints as USAID chief and Foreign Disaster Assistance chief. New Hampshire H. W. Bush campaign leader, US cabinet secretary, and former White House Chief of Staff Andy Card, who was a Republican, taught me how to "be humble, work hard, and be visible!" US congressman and the best friend of Speaker of the House Tip O'Neill at the time, the late Silvio Conte, a liberal Republican, with aides Patrick Larkin and Bob Goudy, taught a young intern in Congress how the federal legislative process works as a ranking minority member on the Appropriations Committee. Meanwhile, not your average Latin American customer and dictator, the late Cuban President Fidel Castro, a Communist-Socialist, is a separate matter in his own right. (*Economicos* de *Politicos*-Economics from politics in the Communist-Socialist system.)

I always appreciate engaging with members of Congress, US senators, federal and state officials, state legislators, and governors when they are active listeners. It was beneficial because I am president emeritus of the New England Brown Egg Council and a member of national industry groups, including the United Egg Producers, American Egg Board, United States Poultry and Egg Export Council, and several nonprofits. Meanwhile, Speaker of the House Tip O'Neill's son, the former Massachusetts lieutenant governor, is an extremely effective lobbyist and damage control expert, as noted earlier in this book. Tom O'Neill, who is a Democrat, demonstrates performance excellence in all that his firm does. Similar appreciation goes to presidential campaign power broker and attorney Jerry Crawford, an Iowa Democrat, and Phil Olsson, a

Republican of OFW Law, and his great partners in Washington, including David Durkin.

Athletes from my alma mater, Tufts, former US senator and former US ambassador Scott Brown, a Republican and former state senator from South Boston, Jack "Jackie" Hart, a Democrat, successfully pulled off some significant victories for themselves and others. How did Scott Brown win Democrat-entrenched South Boston to take Ted Kennedy's seat? I apologize, Scott. I mean "the people's seat." One of the best political comeback lines ever in a political debate came from a former Tufts athlete, Downtown Scotty Brown. He won a close race for US Senate at the buzzer. Speaking of winning elections, you can undoubtedly learn from another Tufts athlete, White House Deputy Chief of Staff Jen O'Malley. She landed in her latest position after pitching a great softball game managing the Joe Biden presidential campaign against a competitor that always threw fast, hard, and right at your head.

Sustainable Leadership and Disruption Podcast Champions: Transforming for a New and Better World in Partnership with Forbes Books

Learning needs to be a continual process. There is no better education than learning from the best in sustainable leadership, innovation, disruption, and growth, and that's why I started a podcast. This podcast is an ongoing learning experience of crushing success focused on exceptional execution around the 12 Principles of Cartel Disruption.

Every month, we highlight a new person on the podcast. These podcast champions have a strong passion for various aspects of sustainability to transform for a new and better world. Guests have included Bob Goehrke and his wife, Tish, on their Inc. 5000 IPG's crushing rise after leaving the cushy corporate life to live near a factory in Salt Lake City, Utah. As noted earlier, John Bello, president of NFL Properties, founder of SoBe, and chairman of Reed's, with creative involvement by his wife, Nancy, and their passion for giving back to Tufts University, was a highlighted guest on the show. In addition, Jack Derby recently gave an impressive $10M gift to the Tufts Entrepreneurship Center that will rename it the Derby Entrepreneurship Center at Tufts in honor of Jack and his wife, Jan. Jack has led an impressive life of technology innovation, consulting, coaching, hard work, teaching, and giving back in a strong and meaningful way.

We heard from Scott Svenson and his wife, Ally's, sustainable mission-based growth with Seattle Coffee and the rocket-ship rise of MOD Pizza and its expansion to hundreds of outlets coast to coast and internationally. Ben Carson Jr. shared how with the backing of his wife, Merlynn, they scaled their minority-

and women-owned venture firms with FVLCRUM Funds and Interprise. They tirelessly give back to the Carson Scholars Fund and many other sustainable causes and civic engagements as part of their desire to transform for a safer, new, and better world. Rodney Herenton of Channing Capital runs a minority-based mutual fund that has had tremendous growth and stellar results with a strong social mission in their blood. As discussed earlier, Joe Meyer was a guest and shared his rocket rides in tech at ExecThread, HopStop (acquired by Apple), and Quigo (acquired by AOL). He shared his passion for giving back by sharing collaborative information on ExecThread and his alma mater, Georgetown. These podcasts and many more are available on DavidRadlo. com and Apple, Spotify, Amazon, Google, or your favorite podcast platform.

Nonprofit Heroes

Chris Nowinski and Dr. Robert Cantu disrupted sports cartels. They raised awareness about safety and improved the lives of people with traumatic brain injuries through the Concussion Legacy Foundation, serving military, civilian-service members, and worldwide former athletes. www.concussionfoundation.org.

In addition, my friends at the New England food banks and others throughout the country have been salvation through Covid-19. Essential workers like my ICU-Neuro CCU fiancée, Anne, the people working to put food on tables through the supply chain, and the great food banks throughout this great nation are heroes.

Team IMPACT deserves mention for their support of children with life-threatening illnesses. Team IMPACT connects sick children and their families with college athletic teams through a "draft" thanks to the leadership of Jay Calnan, Danny Kraft, and their professional management. Imagine having the support of a team of athletes while going through such challenges and difficulties. What an outstanding value proposition that has excellent people, processes, and strategy driving blockbuster growth. The organization was incubated in Boston, accelerated across the country, and now is servicing the world so that children with life-threatening illnesses can benefit from being placed on a college sports team. www.goteamimpact.org.

Boston Globe news legend Frank Phillips, Mary-Jo Adams, and celebrity homebuilder Bob Vila of the Hemingway Preservation Foundation, now called the Finca Vigía Foundation, continue to build bridges between the US and Cuba by preserving Ernest Hemingway's home, artifacts, and boat in Cuba. Great work and worthwhile support! www.fincafoundation.org.

Lastly, I do stand behind Tufts and NYU Stern. They are great educational institutions, and I have been privileged to give time, talents, and money to both. Working together as alumni to turn Tufts into an Athletic Academic Institution focused on sports, fitness, wellness, and student success has been the greatest innovative joy that synergistically works across all undergraduate and graduate schools. www.gotuftsjumbos.com and www.stern.nyu.edu.

Friends of the Catholic Church in Cuba (www.friendsofcaritascubana.org) and the World Jewish Congress in Cuba (www.worldjewishcongress.org) provide essential aid support in Cuba. These people are at the forefront of maintaining the necessities, building bridges, and finding common ground. I am also delighted that the holiday display at the US Embassy in Cuba continues to shine year after year as a beacon of light and hope on the Malecón in Havana.

Sustainably Educating and Supporting Young Minds

I have worked with deans, professors, and professionals to help educate young creative minds on leadership, innovation, and growth at Tufts University and NYU Stern. A few of the exceptional people I have worked with are Kevin Oye, Jack Derby, Tina Weber, Chris Swan, Mike Darling, Ed Saltzman, Dary Mozaffarian, Peter Clay, Ben Carson Jr., Lou "Sweet Lou" Pelosi, Bob "Treibs" Treiber, Jessica Bussgang, and Steve "Zam" Zamierowski.

A former student that I advised and later invested with named Alex Rappaport became the CEO of ZwitterCo. He raised several million dollars in seed and series A round funding. I introduced Alex in Chapters Two and Eleven of *Principles of Cartel Disruption*. ZwitterCo is commercializing and accelerating pollution technology that uses patented technology developed by Tufts University researchers. The technology effectively filters wastewater in commercial settings such as the poultry industry, which sustainably saves water and economic resources. www.zwitterco.com.

In the pitch section of Chapter Two of *Principles for Cartel Disruption*, I discuss Anodyne Nanotech. The company has advanced its Hero Patch platform, which uses a microneedle delivery system in the body for pharmacological doses. They raised $4.2M in seed financing backed by Velocity Partners, Relativity Healthcare Fund, and Big Pi Ventures. The founders, Konstantinos Tzortzakis, Hojat Rezaei Nejad, and Jake Lombardo, did a great job! www.theheropatch.com

It's great when nonprofit organizations appreciate and make use of your time, talents, and finance. The best example is the partnership with student-athletes, coaches, and alumni at Tufts University. A group of us have been thrilled to partner and raise millions of capital for brick, mortar, and support operations. Giving back is more about developing a winning mindset and transforming future leaders than winning national championships, but championships are grand too.

Current sports coaches and professionals at Tufts such as Jay Civetti, John Casey, Bill Gehling, John Morris, Alexis Mastronardi, and Mark "Zig"

Adzigian dedicate their lives to helping kids improve and develop the mindset to achieve. A solid and active alumni base works hard with the coaches for 100% placement after graduation. Usually, there is more demand from alumni than the supply of graduating athletes. www.gotuftsjumbos.com/landing.

Pardon for the drill-down example into fishing ponds, but drilling down in your ponds, wherever they may be, is important. Athletic and fraternal alumni Robert "Tish" Tishman keeps us together with an outstanding holiday party year in and year out. Mike Frisoli, the most successful intern that I have ever worked with within the network system, received seventeen job offers after college. His partner, J. R. McDonald, and he incubated the alumni, parent, and athlete programs with football, which spread to other men's and women's sports. Former Vice Chair Daniel "Dots" Doherty, John Bello, Chair Peter Dolan, Brian "Voog" Kavoogian, and Robert "Bobby" Bendetson as trustees have worked with the administration to accelerate the focus of athletics to the forefront of a strong academic university and stick their necks out to improve the fraternal and sorority system!

I was privileged to go to school with successful women athletes who continued in sports-related activities that have incubated and accelerated to stratospheric levels, including Mary Halladay, Cecelia Wilcox, and Nancy and Lisa Stern. Then again, the Hollywood crew added some interesting spice to life as well: Actor Hank Azaria who is well known for his Simpson's character voices; Jimmy Kimmel's lead writer and comedian Gary "Hammering Hank" Greenberg, whom I played football with; singer-songwriter Tracy Chapman, who performed at times on campus on Wednesday and Thursday nights; and my fraternity brother and fellow football player, *Two and a Half Men* producer Eric Tannenbaum. My time spent in Hollywood is subject to coming attractions for a future book.

Working together as a team to support critical, practical, and sustainable education is tremendously effective and rewarding. As a group, we love spending our time, talents, and money to accelerate performance!

Conrad Challenge, NASA, and SAFE:

Testing the 12 Principles of Cartel Disruption with young high school students proved their validity! I had the privilege of mentoring and coaching a winning team of young high school students that participated in the Conrad Challenge at NASA (www.conradchallenge.org). The students were willing to incubate and accelerate their project based upon these principles. As mentioned in Chapter Eleven of *Principles of Cartel Disruption*, SAFE (Sound the Alternate Fire Extinguisher) is a patent-pending technology that puts out fires with sound waves with metamaterials (www.safefire.tech). The team had benefited from Tina, Jack, and Kevin's summer accelerator program at Tufts University (www.

EXHIBIT AF.1.

From PCD: Photo 11.B.

gordon.tufts.edu) and the good graces of expert patent attorneys and former Tufts athletes, including Doug Kline of Goodwin Proctor and Rich Giunta of Wolf Greenfeld.

After Winning the Conrad Challenge at NASA, graduating seniors from Title 1, Nashua South, have launched their careers, with Jeffrey Lam going to Dartmouth and Ady Shankur going to Stanford. Meanwhile, Josh Gao and Sam Greenberg have rolled up their sleeves and keep working the business by effectively raising money with the aid of the Tufts Venture Accelerator. Sri Korantla has recently joined to assist the efforts. Go get 'em, guys!

Notable Disruption and Accelerating Family Members

The late, great former New York Bar president, Uncle Boris Kostelanetz, would use the lawyerly phrase, "Notwithstanding the foregoing." I was fortunate to have some outstanding creative disruptors in my family who gave service to this great nation. My dad, Jack, was a decorated WWII veteran under George S. Patton. He fought in the European Theatre from the Battle of the Bulge, over the Remagen Bridge, and through the Danube River while under enemy fire. My dad was with Allies who liberated a concentration camp, and he accepted the surrender of several hundred German officers, some of whom he interrogated. My dad had life-long PTSD, which he said he received when Patton ordered the infantry to advance before the mechanized detachments into strong German defenses at the Ruhr Pocket, but he never complained about it. My dad later pioneered Brown Eggs fresh from New England with the advertising jingle, "Brown Eggs Are Local Eggs, and Local Eggs Are Fresh." My dad was a strong agricultural entrepreneur that participated in and led many different agriculture and ag-biotech-related ventures. Jack was recognized and awarded the Urner Barry Man of the Year award for his outstanding service.

My Uncle Bob Frank, a former US Air Force officer, pioneered a new and better way to buy media. He had some notable clients, such as Mike Jeans, while running Beatrice/Hunt-Wesson and the Committee to Re-elect the President (Richard Nixon), and other Republican organizations. As a true capitalist, Bob told me that he tried to get the Democrats' accounts first and failed, so he went after the Republicans. Bob is best at maintaining strong life-long friendships, including with his classmate at Brookline (MA) High School, Mike Dukakis, the former Democratic governor from Massachusetts, and many other very fine people he has kept as friends. Bob also had some great original productions for television. My favorite was *Superstars*, where professional athletes competed in other sports.

Meanwhile, from my father's side, my grandmother Anna and family helped get the test market started on the Lower East Side of New York for her Uncle Zach Zechnowitz, the Swee-Touch-Nee tea creator. The tea can still be purchased today at your local grocery store. My sister Margie is an expert at ag-biotech marketing and management and quite skilled at accelerating at large companies and small and is a woman-supportive angel investor. My sister

AF.2. *Jack Radlo at the End of World War II in 1945 after accepting the surrender of several hundred enemy officers and* **AF.3.** *with my son, Ben, and me at a Patriots Day Parade in Lexington, MA, circa 2000.*

159

Sally is a pioneering expert professor and attorney on everything regarding children involved with the entertainment industry. With appreciation, I want to note Lt. Carl Radlo, who gave the ultimate sacrifice for our nation over the skies of Italy in World War II, disrupting Nazi aggression.

To segue into the sunset, I want to pay tribute to Grandma's other brother, Great Uncle Andre Kostelanetz. He earned a star for his recording activity on the Hollywood Walk of Fame at 6542 Hollywood Boulevard. Uncle Andre created what is known today as easy listening music. He was a commissioner of new works and best known for working with colleagues in the creative process as an orchestra conductor, arranger, and pianist. On conducting and focus, he said in *Echoes: Memoirs of Andre Kostelanetz*, "From the moment that I raise the baton, there is nothing in my mind but the music. It weaves a connection

AF.4. *Picture of Bob Frank, Boris Kostelanetz, Dick Kostelanetz (Boris's son), and Andre Kostelanetz in Israel in the 1970s.*

between me and the orchestra, an invisible web of fabulous intricacy. Only the final applause dissolves the connection and restores us to our physical surroundings."[18] The gratifying applause was the key metric of assurance of achievement.

Further, he worked with CBS Radio on incubating and accelerating the consumption of music via radio to the American consumer in the twentieth century, which he characterized as a process that requires "the closest attention to the smallest detail."[19] This was cited in the summary for the Library of Congress "Andre Kostelanetz Collection." At the start of WWII, he realized that it was best to collaborate with the best for this country's patriotic benefit, such as his commission of the "Great Americans" musical portraits, with Aaron Copland composing Lincoln's portrait and Jerome Kern composing Mark Twain's.

Before country sensation and military-performing champion Toby Keith was born, Uncle Andre led the charge giving back to troops overseas. He conducted over a hundred concerts during WWII on two tours with the USO to the Persian Gulf, North Africa, Italy, Burma, China, and the European Theatre. So the fact that I found a Kostelanetz record spinning in Ernest Hemingway's Cuban home was a lovely tribute to him from arguably one of the best writers in history.

I can personally testify that listening to my uncle's concerts in Lincoln Center as he conducted the New York Philharmonic was awesome at a young age. He believed in collaborating and performing with the best to make the best music always. Leonard Bernstein, Luciano Pavarotti, and Itzhak Perlman were a few that I witnessed. Listen for yourself on Spotify or Amazon, or please Google Andre Kostelanetz on the web for the Library of Congress collection or more information.

With Uncle Andre, or "Kosty," lightly playing in the background ushering in the sunset, I hope you have enjoyed *Secret Stories of Leadership, Growth, and Innovation: Sustainable Transformation for a Safer, New, and Better World.* It's mojito cocktail hour! With hummus-filled stuffed egg whites and cranberry jelly on the deck of Point Del Sol in Cape Cod, there is a light breeze off the water, and the sun is setting. From 4–8 p.m. in the spring, summer, and fall, it's the place to be if you're not playing golf.

Hasta la *vista*!!!

David

Davidradlo.com

About the Author:

David Radlo is an internationally recognized expert in Sustainable Leadership, Growth, and Innovation. He is an accomplished CEO, Outside Director, Trusted Advisor, Growth and Exit Coach, and Fortune 500 speaker. His twenty-eight years as a CEO include delivering a six-fold EBITDA increase and a thirty-fold increase in enterprise value. He is a 3X entrepreneur, which includes organically developing and accelerating multi-billion-dollar consumer specialty eggs and dairy categories with his partners, including Eggland's Best Cage Free, Born Free Range, and private label lines along with Mycotoxin Diagnostics. He also did well on real estate ventures. Radlo has an uncanny ability to find a path for profitable growth, CAGR, and the ability to envision synergistic partnerships, alliances, and organic and inorganic targeted growth initiatives.

He is presently a partner with RB Markets-Achievemost and partner to biotech, agriculture, consumer, franchise, government contracts, entertainment, real estate, and technology businesses. In addition, he has worked on $2.3 billion in acquisitions, both on the buy and sell side. Radlo is experienced in the US and globally, working with private equity firms, private companies, family businesses, venture firms, and executives. In addition, he personally negotiated an agreement with Fidel Castro.

Radlo is a Masters Professional Outside Director (ACCD) and member of ACG. He is an International Fortune 500 Speaker, best-selling author, and ForbesBooks author. His podcast, *Sustainable Leadership and Disruptive Growth*, brings continued education and insight to the industry. In addition, he speaks at corporate and organization engagements as well as at lectures and seminars at Tufts University and NYU Stern School of Business. Radlo integrates the 12 Principles from his books into his teachings to accelerate the audience's organizational and executive performance.

After a rewarding experience educationally and as player for the football program at Tufts University, Radlo later became a recruiter while coaching with the longest-serving high school football coach in America. He bridged his experiential learning at Tufts with a five-year career in public service, political advocacy, and working with the US Congress and Massachusetts General Court. He subsequently ran a strong race for state representative, receiving 39% of the votes, commencing as a senior in college, and received an endorsement from Vice President George H. W. Bush. Radlo worked for H. W. Bush in his 1988 presidential campaign, turned down potential opportunities at the White House and State Department, and finally turned to the traditional business sector. He accepted a management position with Citibank to spearhead the marketing and sales for their equivalent of Western Union. He left Citibank to enter NYU Stern for his MBA and later worked for Chase.

Radlo took a management role in a consumer-agriculture and ag-biotech company and later founded Radlo Foods, a company entrenched in brown, specialty, domestic, and international commodity eggs, wholesale food distribution, specialty foods, and a partnership in biotech with Vicam. At Vicam, they advanced food safety and partnered with MIT, Harvard, BU, and Johns Hopkins.

Fast-forward a decade; the biotech company was sold to a strategic partner at a high enterprise value. At Radlo Foods, Radlo expanded operations to thirty states and reached out to EMEA, Canada, the Caribbean, and Asia Pacific. As a result, the company footprinted and replicated specialty designer eggs and products that exploded the category through segmentation, creating two national brands and several private-label brands that led to YOY double-digit growth. In addition, Radlo was adept at fostering appropriate add-on acquisitions. He then sold his Eggland's Best ownership and franchise to Land O'Lakes for substantial enterprise value. Radlo has served on all committees of the American Egg Board and the USA Poultry and Egg Export Council, where he helped shape US trade policy. He was also president of the New England Brown Egg Council.

His board and advisory experience include Fulcrum Private Equity, Charlesbank Capital Partners, QC Agri Supply, Radlo Foods (Egg-Land's Best and Born Free), Vicam Biotech, NRI Cannabis Parkinson's Biotechnology, and Hollywood and Me Entertainment Ventures. His nonprofit boards and advisory roles have included: the Concussion Legacy Foundation; several Tufts University-related boards and advisory positions in nutrition, innovation, athletics, fraternal, and veterinary; the Hemingway Preservation Foundation (Finca Vigía Foundation); support for several charities in addition to the above, including Team Impact, local food banks, the Jewish Distribution Committee in Cuba, and Caritas Cubana (Catholic Charities in Cuba) as well as support for US troops fighting overseas and the US Embassy (Cuba) holiday display.

He has degrees from Tufts and NYU and received an honorary degree from Boston College. Radlo is a certified management consultant and growth coach. He has a US patent pending and twenty-one trademarks assigned. He resides in the Boston area, is engaged to Anne Winkler, an ICU-CCU Trauma One Social Worker, and enjoys watching his kids develop their business, leadership, management, and communication skills. With whatever time remains, he takes walks and runs at Point Del Sol, enjoying his home at the Cape, snowshoeing in New England, and getting in some rounds of golf.

For more information, please go to DavidRadlo.com

Notes

1. English, T. J. *Havana Nocturne: How the Mob Owned Cuba . . . and then Lost It to the Revolution.* New York: William Morrow, 2008, p. 161.

2. English, *Havana Nocturne*, p. 275.

3. Frank, Marc. *Cuban Revelations: Behind the Scenes in Havana.* Gainesville: University Press of Florida, 2013, pp. 19–20.

4. Frank, *Cuban Revelations*, p. 15.

5. Rutenborg, Jan. *Tourism Apartheid and Sustainable Ground Level Tourism. A Study of Tourism Policy and Its Implications on Society in Cuba.* Master's thesis, Stockholm University. Stockholm: Institution for Latin-American Studies, 2020.

6. Frank, *Cuban Revelations*, p. 34.

7. O'Grady, Mary Anastasia. "Opinion | Behind Cuba's Covid Uprising." *Wall Street Journal.* July 11, 2021. Accessed July 14, 2021. https://www.wsj.com/articles/behind-cubas-covid-uprising-11626042703.

8. Mendez, Samara. *USDA Analytics-United Egg Producers 2016.* PDF. Rockville: The Humane League Labs, August 11, 2019.

9. Chesto, Jon. "Egg Industry Warns of Shortage in Mass. without Legislative Action." *Boston Globe.* BostonGlobe.com. March 06, 2021. Accessed July 04, 2021. https://www.bostonglobe.com/2021/03/06/business/egg-industry-warns-shortage-mass-without-legislative-action/.

10. Chesto, Jon. "Egg Industry Warns of Shortage in Mass. without Legislative Action."

11. "Better Meat Co. Announces Mycoprotein Fermentation Facility." Accessed August 04, 2021. https://www.bettermeat.co/news/the-better-meat-co-announces-completion-of-fermentation-plant-to-produce-mycoprotein-superfood.

12. Shapiro, Paul. *Clean Meat: How Growing Meat without Animals Will Revolutionize Dinner and the World.* New York, NY: Gallery Books, 2018, p. 225.

13. Gates, Bill. *How to Avoid a Climate Disaster: The Solutions We Have and the Breakthroughs We Need.* New York, NY: Alfred A. Knopf, 2020, p. 225.

14. Crawford, Elizabeth. "'Carbon Score Is the Next Big Thing,' Predicts CGC Co-head, Industry Experts Gathered by FoodBytes!" *Foodnavigator*. May 13, 2021. Accessed August 04, 2021. https://www.foodnavigator-usa.com/Article/2021/05/13/Carbon-score-is-the-next-big-thing-predicts-CGC-co-head-industry-experts-gathered-by-FoodBytes.

15. Grant, Adam M. *Give and Take: Why Helping Others Drives Our Success*. New York: Penguin Books, 2014.

16. Smith, Hedrick. *The Power Game: How Washington Works*. New York: Ballantine Books, 1996, p.160.

17. Schwantes, Marcel. "Warren Buffett Says All Successful Leaders Have 1 Thing in Common." Inc.com. January 22, 2021. Accessed July 04, 2021. https://www.inc.com/marcel-schwantes/warren-buffett-says-all-successful-leaders-have-one-thing-in-common.html.

18. Kostelanetz, Andre, and Gloria Hammond. *Echoes: Memoirs of Andre Kostelanetz*. New York: Houghton Mifflin Harcourt, 1981, p. 215.

19. "Estate of Andre Kostelanetz." Charles H. Weinberg to Mr. Nathan R. Einhorn. September 9, 1980. New York.

Lightning Source UK Ltd.
Milton Keynes UK
UKHW020736310822
408116UK00009B/737